P9-DWA-326

AN ANATOMY OF
The Turn of the Screw

AN ANATOMY OF
The Turn of the Screw

By THOMAS MABRY CRANFILL
and ROBERT LANIER CLARK, JR.

UNIVERSITY OF TEXAS PRESS, AUSTIN

Library of Congress Catalog Card Number 65-13514
Copyright © 1965 by Thomas M. Cranfill and Robert L. Clark, Jr.
All Rights Reserved

Printed in the United States of America
by The University of Texas Printing Division, Austin
Bound by Universal Bookbindery, Inc., San Antonio

For Betty Cranfill Wright

PREFACE

The Turn of the Screw first conscripted my imagination (to borrow Heywood Broun's phrase describing the power of the work) twenty years ago when, after teaching it to three classes of freshmen, I began to set down my views of the tale. These might have had to await publication even longer had I not had the good fortune to enlist my nephew Robert L. Clark, Jr., as a collaborator, my own burning interest in the story having infected him so thoroughly that he wrote his M.A. thesis on the topic.

Though both of us have had a hand in all parts of this study, to him belongs most of the credit for plowing with patience, thoroughness, and discrimination through the vast critical commentary on Henry James. His findings, recorded in the Selected Bibliography, of course broadened our perspective and enriched our own study of the tale. For the interpretation of James's text and for the writing of this volume I must be held largely accountable, though my coauthor's improvements in organization and style may be found on many a page.

Thanks to the Bibliography, no footnotes litter the bottom margins of this book or lurk at the ends of chapters to leap out at the reader. He may, if interested in pursuing a quotation, a reference, or an idea, find the requisite information in the Bibliography. This list, please observe, has been carefully entitled "A Selected Bibliography." No scholar in his right mind would pretend to have gleaned every last comment on James and his masterpiece any more than to have canvased all the critiques concerning *Hamlet*. We nevertheless hope that we have recorded the most interesting and important ones.

At the outset it seemed that sixty years of critical utterances, 1898–1958, would be enough to take into account. Then in 1959 Ingrid Bergman starred in a television show as James's governess; in 1961 Deborah Kerr did likewise in the movies; and in 1962 Benjamin Britten's operatic treatment of *The Turn of the Screw* was one of the New York Center's offerings for the season. Since all three productions provoked further comments, we included a few of the most stimulating in the Bibliography, plus a handful of critiques of 1963 and 1964, until at last additions were no longer possible.

Throughout this study we quote and refer to Leon Edel's reprint of *The Turn of the Screw* as James revised it for inclusion in the 1908 edition of his collected works. The reprint appears in Edel's edition of *The Ghostly Tales of Henry James* (New Brunswick, Rutgers University Press, 1948).

For counsel and encouragement I am grateful to my colleague Professor Willis W. Pratt and for help in preparing the manuscript for publication to my friends and former students Hans Beacham, William J. Johnson, and Magdalena B. Sumpter. Finally, I am indebted to the University of Texas Research Institute for a research leave in 1960 that furthered the writing of this book.

T. M. C.

The University of Texas

CONTENTS

AN ANATOMY OF
The Turn of the Screw

I. *Introduction*

IF SCOPE, variety, and abundance of critical comments are tests of the quality of a book, then Henry James's *The Turn of the Screw* (1898) is a deathless work of art. The student of these critiques finds himself recalling shelf upon shelf groaning under commentaries on *Hamlet*. He further reflects that *Hamlet* has been available for comment for about three hundred and sixty-six years, *The Turn of the Screw* for only sixty-six. That critics will bring their remarks on James's story to an end during this century, or the next, appears unlikely. Like *Hamlet*, *The Turn of the Screw* is both a masterpiece and a problem.

It first came out in weekly installments in *Collier's,* January 27 to April 16, 1898, then in book form in a volume called *The Two Magics,* also published in 1898. Critiques of the story began appearing immediately and have continued until, presumably, day before yesterday. From the first the tale attracted a truly astonishing variety of critics, novelists, short-story writers, essayists, scholars, editors, humorists, poets, drama critics, literary critics (Old and New), social historians, journalists, memoirists, students of the technique of fiction writing, students of psychiatry, students of psychical research—all have had their say. Their utterances have filled the pages of periodicals as diverse as *Time* and *Newsweek, The Kenyon Review, The University of Kansas City Review,* and *The Sewanee Review,* and the *PMLA.* A prime indication of the power of James's work is that it has commanded attention from nearly all cultural strata.

Not all of these can be explored here since the principal business of our book is a careful analysis of the tale itself. But to those who want to trace in detail its fate at the hands of the humble and the renowned alike and to learn how broad are its dimensions and how multifarious its facets, our Bibliography with symbols indicating the contents of scores of critiques should prove useful. Before studying James's text, we intend to treat only the two parts of the critical background which are most important to an appreciation of our own investigation.

The strife between Big Endians and Little Endians or between Shakespeareans and Baconians has been scarcely more heated, bitter, and prolonged than what Oliver Evans calls "the distinguished discord between the apparitionist and nonapparitionist readers of *The Turn of the Screw.*" The apparitionists, who far outnumber their foes, consider the governess a victim of supernatural visitations, while the nonapparitionists think she suffers from some sort of mental derangement, maybe from hallucinations. A few voices from both camps, chosen because of their chronology, typicality, persuasiveness, or réclame, deserve a hearing. First the apparitionists.

"The story is concerned with the malign influence exercised on two exquisite and brilliant children . . . by two dead servants," states Pelham Edgar. According to Charles G. Hoffman, the "ghosts are real, and the children are corrupt and evil." F. R. Leavis considers Quint and Miss Jessel "the consistently bad ghosts of bad persons," and Elizabeth Stevenson discerns in the character of the governess "just the right note of limited common sense and propriety to furnish the necessary foil to the other and unnatural note of impropriety and horror in Miss Jessel, Peter Quint, Flora, and little Miles." Robert Heilman is "convinced that . . . the story means exactly what it says: that at Bly there are apparitions which the governess sees, which Mrs. Grose does not see but comes to believe in . . . and of which the children have a knowledge which they endeavor to conceal."

These remarks by five apparitionists pretty well epitomize what Edna Kenton in 1924 called the "traditional, we might almost call it a *lazy* version of the tale" of "children hounded by prowling ghosts." The excerpts from apparitionist views could be extended for pages, for the roster is long, yet the tale had hardly seen print before two readers in 1898 came close to impugning the governess' sanity, an anonymous reviewer for *The Critic* of December 1898, and Oliver Elton: the latter confesses a "doubt, raised and kept hanging, whether, after all, the two ghosts who can choose to which persons they will appear, are facts, or delusions of the young governess who tells the story."

In 1919 Henry A. Beers, writing on Hawthorne, characterizes the apparitions in *The Turn of the Screw* as "just a suspicion of evil presences. The true interpretation of that story I have sometimes thought to be, that the woman who saw the phantoms was mad."

Until recently Edna Kenton's essay in *The Arts* for November 1924 was generally regarded as the earliest nonapparitionist provocation of the debate between the two schools. Actually her views were anticipated, though not in print, by the late Harold C. Goddard, whose "A Pre-Freudian Reading of *The Turn of the Screw*" dates from about 1920 if not before, according to his daughter. His thorough, measured analysis of the story appeared in June 1957 as the lead article of the special James issue of *Nineteenth-Century Fiction*. As complete as any nonapparitionist statement we have seen, Goddard's study copes in detail with several major cruxes in the novel, including Mrs. Grose's identification of Quint, the scenes by the lake, and the final catastrophe. In the judgment of Leon Edel, who supplies a preface to the essay, Goddard provides a valuable example of textual study. He read his interpretation to generations of Swathmore students, never failing to find "the majority of my fellow readers ready to prefer it to their own."

As Edel points out in his preface to Goddard's article, Edna Kenton in "Henry James to the Ruminant Reader," in 1924, was the first to call attention in print to the importance of point of view in the tale, where the action is seen entirely through the governess' eyes. For Miss Kenton, not "the children, but the little governess was hounded by the ghosts," and the prologue casts "the only light we have on her present or her past—her whole concern is with the children and the ghosts. But of these we have only her story, and we have got nowhere near 'the story of the story' until, pressing resolutely through her irresistibly credible recounting of the horrors at Bly, we come into closer quarters with the secret causes of her admirable *flair* for the evil she finds there."

Thanks to her irresistibly credible narrative, the apparitionist approach to the tale "has come down through a quarter of a century of readers' reactions resulting from 'a cold, artistic calculation' on the part of its highly entertained author." As for the governess, the "eager, thrilled, horrified reader, joined with her in her vivid hunt after hidden sins, has failed to think sufficiently of her."

Most apparitionists complain that Edmund Wilson thought too persistently, and wrongheadedly, of the governess as he prepared "The Ambiguity of Henry James" (1934), by all odds the most widely read, replied-to, or agreed-with of commentaries on the story, if not on James himself. The gist of his argument is that in the novel "almost everything from beginning to end can be read equally in either of two senses." In the sense in which he prefers to construe the plot, Wilson envisages the governess as not merely the narrator, but as the victim of neurotic sex repression as well—one of James's frustrated spinsters. What is more, he believes "the whole story has been primarily intended as a characterization of the governess." He cites certain Freudian symbols in the story and James's failure to include it among his other tales on ghostly themes. Instead, he consigned it to a volume of stories of another kind.

One cannot overrate the effect which Wilson's essay has produced on both camps. Let us consider how Edel has amplified the last argument mentioned. In "The Architecture of Henry James's 'New York Edition'," Edel discusses James's placement of *The Turn of the Screw*, not with his ghostly tales in Volume XVII, but between *The Aspern Papers* and "The Liar." The former and *The Turn of the Screw* thus stand "side by side—'Tales of Curiosity'—the curious 'publishing scoundrel' seeking to pry the secrets of Aspern from Juliana, the curious governess seeking at all costs to tear out of Bly its extraordinary secrets that reside in her mind. (It is certainly no coincidence that the story James placed immediately beside *The Turn of the Screw* was *The Liar*)." Instead of coincidence, Edel sees conscious intention in the placement, quoting a letter from James to Scribner, his publisher, insisting that his groupings were "exceedingly considered and various congruities and affinities much observed, so that each volume should offer, as to content, a certain harmonious physiognomy."

But Edel is in the minority. The majority have interested themselves not so much in the pursuit and amplification of Wilson's theories as in their refutation. In the opinion of E. E. Stoll the fact that only one person sees a ghost does not constitute an adequate argument against the apparitionist theory, for "this is the way of ghosts in general." Without ghosts Oliver Evans finds "no evil, no danger, no exposure" in the tale; without the "possession theme, which necessitates the reality of the ghosts, there is simply no conflict, no drama, no *story*." A. J. A. Waldock is unable to conceive how the governess can project "on vacancy, out of her own subconscious mind, a perfectly precise . . . image of a man, then dead, whom she had never seen in her life and never heard of."

On the other hand, Wilson's hypothesis strikes Yvor Winters as "more plausible than the popular one." In James's *The American,* Winters sees "a marked tendency . . . on the part of James and of his characters alike to read into situations more than can be justified by the facts as given, to build up intense states of feeling, on the basis of such reading, and to judge or act as a result of that feeling. This . . . is what we found the governess doing in *The Turn of the Screw,* so intensely, in fact, that the story may well be taken to serve, if we accept the psychopathic interpretation, as a very acute and devastating self-parody."

Osborn Andreas proposes that the "governess in *The Turn of the Screw* . . . subjects Flora and Miles . . . to all the vagaries of her progressively more and more deranged mind," so that we have here the "harrowing story of the obsessive and rapacious emotional devouring of two innocent children by an emotionally avid governess" whose "only motive is the satisfaction of her emotional need." As the tone of these remarks shows, Wilson's interpretation enlisted no more fiery or vehement a nonapparitionist convert than this commentator.

William York Tindall also focuses his study on the governess. "In *The Turn of the Screw*," he writes, "James, an expert in the unmentionable, used all his arts of indirection. The story is told in first person by the governess not only because the ambiguities must not be injured by intervention of the author but because, an apparent neurotic, she must be allowed to expose the workings of her mind, upon which in the end our interest must center."

No treatment of apparitionists and nonapparitionists would seem adequate without mention of the disagreement between F. R. Leavis and Marius Bewley that enlivens the pages of *Scrutiny* in 1950. Their critical altercation amounts almost to a flyting. It begins with Bewley's "Appearance and Reality in Henry James," where he cites James's own remark prefacing the New York edition that the apparitions are "evoked," a term which "posits a real relation between the demons and someone living at Bly, and . . . the person is the governess and not the children." Miles and Flora "are presented to us entirely through the governess' words, and she is 'a mistress of shades'." Bewley also contends that "the governess never has any facts about Miles or Flora to deduce a case from. What she offers is a tissue of surmises built upon the slenderest possible quantity of evidence." "For what are the demons," he inquires, "but objective symbols of the governess's distorted 'moral sense'?" He concludes: "It is, then, the governess who is possessed."

In his rebuttal, "James's 'What Maisie Knew'," Leavis takes issue with Bewley's remarks on *The Turn of the Screw*: "The 'ambiguity' that Mr. Bewley examines . . . is created, it seems to me, by Mr. Bewley himself, and I find the ingenuity of the creating, the way in which he arrives at his 'evoked' demons . . . astonishingly perverse." Leavis believes that the soundest refutation of Bewley's contentions is simply to "read the story itself."

In "Maisie, Miles, and Flora, the Jamesian Innocents," Bewley offers a number of direct ripostes to Leavis's remarks and seizes the opportunity to add still another nonapparitionist assertion: "I believe that the effectiveness of *The Turn of the Screw,* its haunting and disturbing quality, arises from the fact that the reader uneasily suspects that he is aiding and abetting the governess in her persecution of the children."

Leavis appends a very short note to the end of Bewley's essay, once again questioning several of the nonapparitionist points, but concluding resignedly, "I must not take up the argument again. I find . . . nothing 'metaphysically appalling' in *The Turn of the Screw*: Mr. Bewley and I have not shaken one another. We must submit the case to others."

After this brief, only partial résumé of both critical positions, the least one can say of Wilson's celebrated study is that it is provocative. The most unconvinced apparitionist evidently does not regard it as beneath consideration. It therefore seems ironical that the critic who had so much to do with generating the distinguished discord subsequently retreated, though he did not precisely recant. Writing in *The New Yorker* in 1944, he recapitulates the nonapparitionist position, but adds, "it is probable that James was unconscious of having raised something more frightening than the ghosts he had contemplated."

Still, this résumé ends on a note of cheer for nonapparitionists who, after valiantly following Wilson's lead, must have felt daunted by his near-surrender. Invited to add a postscript to his famous essay before its inclusion in Gerald Willen's *A Casebook on Henry James's "The Turn of the Screw,"* Wilson once again seized the banner and waved it. His postscript, dated 1959, begins, "Since writing the above, I have become convinced that James knew exactly what he was doing and that he intended the governess to be suffering from delusions."

Critics embroiled on both sides in the discord just rehearsed have appealed for support to what James himself revealed about his intentions concerning the story. Some impression of those intentions, it is argued, may be gathered from the author's deeds as well as from his words, spoken and written. As the preceding discussion shows, Wilson and Edel contend that what James did about placing the story in his collected works indicates what kind of story he had intended to confect. According to Edel, James *did* something revelatory again when he revised the tale for inclusion in the New York edition. These revisions will receive comment shortly.

It is a blessing that, to some, at least, actions speak louder than words, for apparitionist and nonapparitionist seldom agree how to construe James's explanations. In his preface to the edition of 1908 James deprecates his tale as "a piece of ingenuity pure and simple, of cold artistic calculation, an *amusette* to catch those not easily caught . . . the jaded, the disillusioned, the fastidious." What precisely did James mean by this pronouncement? The cold artistic calculation "on the part of its highly entertained author" misled apparitionists into their traditional, lazy interpretation of the work as a mere ghost story, says Edna Kenton.

But her interpretation and even her method outrage Oliver Evans, who pronounces James's preface "invaluable for the light which it throws on his intentions"—that is, to ensnare the blasé with a powerful ghost story. He writes, "Miss Kenton has not ignored this preface; she has done what is far worse: she has lifted one of its sentences out of its context, interpreted it in a very special kind of way, and then . . . proceeded to construct upon it her very largest argument. In the case of a writer such as James, where context is almost all-important, this is particularly reprehensible." In his gloss on the same passage by James, E. E. Stoll agrees with Evans: James meant "not catching the readers in a trap but capturing their attention and interest." To Stoll, a "detective story *The Turn of the Screw* is not."

Earl Roy Miner praises another apparitionist, Robert Heilman, because he put "the remarks from the Preface back in their proper context." Similarly, Carl Van Doren has great respect for James's statement of intentions, which he finds consistent with the author's performance in the actual story. Van Doren castigates nonapparitionist critics so wrapped up in their own ingenious and imaginative readings that they miss the (apparitionist) point of the story "in spite of James's own scrupulously clear account of what he had in mind to do and what he did." Van Doren continues with the orthodox apparitionist interpretation of James's statements and performance. "He thought of the ghosts as demons from the pit," and the governess he "desired . . . to serve solely as the lens through which the action could be seen, without refraction or coloring. . . . The narrator must be lost sight of in the narration."

Morris Roberts admits that "the story can be read as a case history of hallucination, probably Freudian," and that this "may be the right story, the one James intended, although his preface is completely against this view." In other words, Roberts does not share Van Doren's convictions that James's prefatory remarks necessarily preclude the non-apparitionist reading. These convictions, however, apparently *are* shared by Ferner Nuhn, who writes, "James was often enough indirect, but deliberate misstatement for the purpose of throwing his readers off the track is, I believe, out of character."

Where such critics find straightforwardness, scrupulous clarity, and consistency of stated intentions with actual performance, others find the opposite. Edna Kenton was not the first nor the last to ascribe to James a certain wiliness. Neither Anna Leach in 1916 nor Graham Greene twenty years later was able to accept the tale as a kind of Christmas carol. "James casually mentioned that he wrote the thing as a 'Christmas story'!" Anna Leach exclaims. Greene asserts that when James is dealing with the fear of spiritual evil "he treats the reader with less than his usual frankness: 'a fairy tale pure and simple,' something seasonable for Christmas, is a disingenuous description of *The Turn of the Screw.*"

Just as Miss Kenton in 1924 believes that James not only misled the unwary but was highly entertained by his deception, G. C. Knight in 1925 inquires, "Has James, laughing up his sleeve the while, composed only a very novel ghost story?" Leo B. Levy also suspects James of exercising his sense of humor and speculates that the apparitionist-non-apparitionist debate would have delighted the author just as it does readers.

Among the most temperate judgments of critics familiar with James's remarks are those of F. W. Dupee and John Mason Brown. Dupee comments that James "wrote and said many conflicting things about the story." Brown, like Morris Roberts, finds the nonapparitionist reading "a reasonable enough interpretation. . . . It may even be the right one, though no one really knows, since Henry James failed to be explicit about his intentions."

Philip Rahv proposes an explanation for James's failure to be explicit: "In writing his bogey-tale James succeeded so well in conveying a sense of dreadful and unguessable things that upon its publication . . . he found himself answering questions that apparently he preferred not to answer. . . . to judge by the vagueness and coyness of his replies, James was deliberately trying to choke off the discussion." If so, James failed dismally—how dismally the interested reader can estimate by consulting the flood of additional apparitionist and nonapparitionist discussions of James's intentions and performance cited in our bibliography.

The dissension which, as James might have put it, gleams and glooms above is enough to tempt one to pass over James's own comments on his novel. But only the conscienceless or superficial would dream of ignoring what an author said about his own story, and James said a great deal, from 1895 to 1908, in conversations, in letters, in his notebooks, and in the prefaces he prepared for the New York edition.

Scholars who want to read every word of his often lengthy and intricate remarks are, again, referred to the bibliography. But whoever expects, by perusing them all, in chronological or any other order, to gain unequivocal elucidation is too optimistic. His perusal may lead him to echo Byron's cry after reading Coleridge's *Biographia Literaria*, "I wish he would explain his explanation"—or at the very least to validate Dupee's impression that James wrote and said many conflicting things about the story. Several passages will illustrate both the general tenor of James's explications and his tendency to contradict himself.

How important a work did its author consider *The Turn of the Screw* to be? James's often quoted estimate that it is merely a piece of ingenuity, an *amusette,* is not his only reply to this question. Shortly after its appearance in print he cast doubt on its importance in letters to Louis Waldstein, H. G. Wells, and F. W. H. Myers. To Waldstein he wrote on October 21, 1898: "I am only afraid, perhaps, that my conscious intention strikes you as having been larger than I deserve it should be thought. . . . And as regards a presentation of things so fantastic as in that wanton little Tale, I can only rather blush to see real substance read into them—I mean for the generosity of the reader."

His deprecations continued in letters to Wells and Myers. On December 9, 1898, he assured the former that "the thing is essentially a pot-boiler and a *jeu d'esprit,*" an appraisal he repeated to Myers on December 19 of the same year: "The *T. of the S.* is a very mechanical matter, I honestly think—an inferior, a merely pictorial, subject and rather a shameless pot-boiler." So much for the tenor of his remarks about the story almost immediately after it came out.

He sounded the same note in his preface of 1908, where he labeled the story "this perfectly independent and irresponsible little fiction." Again, "The exhibition involved . . . is a fairy-tale pure and simple." Despite this persistent belittlement, he then proceeded to show in a remarkable way that he did *not* regard the little fiction as negligible. In the same preface he devoted eight finely printed pages—well over three thousand words—to a discussion of it, as compared to the two pages he accorded "The Liar" and "The Two Faces" together, though this pair of tales ends the volume containing *The Turn of the Screw.*

The eight-page discussion of the latter is not only lengthy, but detailed and earnest. To mention some of the matters that James takes up: he boasts of the unity he managed to achieve in the story; he deplores the passing of the really effective, old-fashioned ghost stories— "roughly so to term them"—and the rise of the unpromising new type, "the mere modern 'psychical' case"; he discusses his source and his approach to it; he traces his struggle for clarity, unity, and a reasonable conciseness while at the same time letting his imagination go; he defines the "tone" of the story; he contrasts Quint and Miss Jessel ("not 'ghosts' at all . . . but goblins, elves, imps, demons," etc.) to recorded and attested "ghosts"; he tells how he coped with the problem of evil; he adds what amounts to a short but illuminating essay on the character of his governess.

No short summary can suggest adequately the thoroughness and conscientiousness of James's remarks about the novel's genesis and evolvement. Surely never did an insignificant, irresponsible little fiction, an inferior, merely pictorial subject, and a rather shameless potboiler receive more significant, responsible treatment in a preface by its author.

His essay on the governess' character deserves further notice because it involves another contradiction, explicit rather than implied. To Wells, who had evidently complained that the governess had not been adequately characterized, James replied in his letter of December 9, 1898, that he "had, about my young woman, to take a very sharp line. . . . I had to rule out subjective complications of her own—play of tone, etc.; and keep her impersonal save for the most obvious and indispensable little note of neatness, firmness and courage—without which she wouldn't have had her data."

In the preface, on the other hand, James remembered a reproachful reader "capable evidently, for the time, of some attention, but not quite capable of enough, who complained that I hadn't sufficiently 'characterised' my young woman engaged in her labyrinth; hadn't endowed her with signs and marks, features and humours, hadn't in a word invited her to deal with her own mystery as well as with that of Peter Quint, Miss Jessel and the hapless children."

This complaint provoked a remarkable reaction in James: ". . . one's artistic, one's ironic heart shook for the instant almost to breaking," and he replied that he had to choose among the difficulties which writing the tale presented and concentrate on the greatest. "I saw no way . . . to exhibit her" except in her relationship to the "so many intense anomalies and obscurities" which confronted her. If he had chosen to characterize her further, he would have revealed "her relation to her own nature." Even so, we "have surely as much of her own nature as we can swallow in watching it reflect her anxieties and inductions."

Which of James's explanations should we believe? Did he endow his governess with neatness, firmness, and courage but otherwise leave her impersonal, devoid of subjective complications? Or did he give us quite as much of her own nature as we can swallow, so that his artistic, ironic heart almost quaked to pieces at the injustice of the charge that he had not sufficiently characterized her?

For answers to these questions we recommend turning away from the author's conflicting statements of what he *intended* to do and, applying to the tale that close attention which his critic was unable to pay, repairing to the text to see what James actually *did*. The problem here is that one must repair to two versions of the text, the original and the revised.

II. *Textual Niceties*

EW CRITICS except Leon Edel have had anything to say about the two texts of *The Turn of the Screw*. Nowadays the study of textual niceties is not popular in many circles. The usual practice seems to be to leave such drudgery as collation to the pedant who may be good for little else and thus free one's self to engage the energies, critical faculties, and imagination in pursuing images, allegories, paradoxes, symbols, ironies, ambiguities, theological implications—what not. But is it safe to overlook the considerable revisions the tale underwent before reappearing in the definitive New York edition of 1908—in the form in which James intended finally to leave it?

Those whom Ezra Pound accused of talking pettiness about James's style might have their eyes opened by the scores of conscientious, ingenious, and imaginative changes that James made in the original text of 1898 as he readied it for the New York edition. Practically without exception his alterations are improvements, stylistically and semantically. In perusing them, one should recall again James's pained rejoinder to the accusation of indecently expatiating: *The Turn of the Screw* contains "not an inch of expatiation," James insisted; as he composed it he fought for every grudged inch of space. He carried on the fight in his revisions, rendering dozens of passages more concise.

Clarity as well as conciseness concerned him greatly. He replaced pronouns whose antecedents were not clear, deleted words that verged on the archaic, relieved the text of superfluous punctuation, rendered metaphors consistent, italicized words to make immediately apparent an emphasis he sought, rearranged sentences and simplified word order, and thus clarified his drift. For the elaborate he everywhere substituted simpler words and expressions. He replaced "interlocutor" with "converser," "interlocutress" with "informant," "had beheld" with "had seen," "mounted afresh" with "revived," and "dreadfully austere inquiry" with "straight question enough."

He took pains to introduce strong words in place of the less effective, precise words and phrases in place of the vague, changing "sense" to "grasp," "Yes" to "Never," "see" to "trace," "done" to "administered," "the only thing" to "the one appearance," "thing" to "resource," "most strange manner," to "very high manner," "the business" to "the strain." He was careful to avoid needless verbal and phrasal repetitions, some of them already in the original text, others introduced by his revisions. As he read through his earlier text he apparently noticed that he had overworked "on the spot"; the phrase accordingly several times became something else or disappeared completely. To the extravagant repetition of sounds—to matters of euphony —he was also sensitive, so that he removed such phrases as "weary with watching" and "so terribly suddenly" and put "weary with vigils" and "so terribly all at once" in their place.

That he saw multifarious opportunities to improve the text of 1898 will not surprise those who recall that James dictated it. Not that there is anything weak or careless about the earlier version, stylistically or otherwise. On the contrary, it is a monument to James's powers of concentration and a magnificently effective story. James simply rendered finer an already finely wrought piece of prose. Both versions inspire admiration for James the craftsman, the stylist, the artist. The final version inspires admiration for James the editor as well. He clearly

wanted his collected fiction to include *The Turn of the Screw* in as
highly polished a state as adroit and painstaking revision could yield.
The pains he lavished on the polishing should provide with food for
thought critics who persist in accepting his dismissal of the tale as an
irresponsible little fiction, an inferior subject.

The revisions illuminate much in addition to his lively artistic
conscience. They tell us something about his intentions regarding, first,
the governess' reactions to her experiences and, second, the general
tone of the story. Though the governess impresses one as sufficiently effusive and nerve-wracked in the text of 1898, James set about to in-
tensify her expressions of horror and suffering. Her "grief" of 1898
became her "anguish" of 1908. Similarly, James substituted "the unspeakable minute" for "the minute," "tension" for "excitement,"
"bolt" for "retreat," "turmoil" for "predicament," "wailed" for
"sobbed," "ordeal" for "predicament," "my horrid plunge" for "my
plunge," "my dreadful way" for "my way," and "his dreadful little
mind," for "his little mind."

In his preface to *The Turn of the Screw* James asserted that "the
study is of a conceived 'tone,' the tone of suspected and felt trouble."
Analyzing James's revisions, Leon Edel noticed in his edition of *The
Ghostly Tales* that the changes betrayed James's determination "to alter
the nature of the governess' testimony from that of a report of things
observed, perceived, recalled, to things *felt*." Edel arrived at the conclusion that the tale is primarily a record of feeling. We could not agree
more heartily. Our own study of the text validates Edel's findings, gives
us a wholesome respect for James's prefatory remark, and leads us to
believe that the master meant precisely what he said when he spoke of
"felt" trouble.

Here are a few illustrations of how James reinforced this already conspicuous tone. He changed "I perceived" to "I felt" (twice), "I now
reflect" to "I now feel," and "Mrs. Grose appeared to me" to "Mrs.
Grose affected me." These in addition to the scores of passages in which
the governess had already confided her feelings in the 1898 version.
The result is unmistakable.

In the course of the novel the governess insists that she sees the ghost of the late valet, Peter Quint, four times. In Chapter IX, at the third encounter, in 1898, she writes, "I saw that there was someone on the stair." James amended the sentence to read, "I knew that there was a figure on the stair," the governess' feeling by now having grown sufficiently intense to constitute, for her, knowledge.

In the more than seven printed pages of the prologue in *The Turn of the Screw*, 1908, the word "feel" occurs not once, in any of its forms. But on the very first page of the governess' narrative she begins to use it, in her second sentence, and she continues to use some variant or derivative of it ("feel," "felt," "feeling," "feelings") until her very last page, where it occurs in her penultimate sentence. In all, it appears in her record eighty-two times.

Impressive though these statistics are, they do not tell the whole story. Keeping company with "feel" throughout are other words, repeated over and over, to show that the governess is recording, not what is provable, but what she senses or fancies or feels, how things appear or seem to her. Note the recurrences of some form of the following: "fancy" (used thirteen times), "appear" (eighteen times), "sense" (twenty-one times), "seem" (twenty-three times). Really, her manuscript puts one in mind of the last line of the saucy old limerick,

> There was a Faith Healer of Deal
> Who said, "Although pain isn't real,
> When I sit on a pin, and it punctures my skin,
> I dislike what I fancy I feel."

James wasted no time in giving his reader the clue, as these extracts from Chapter I of the governess' manuscript will show. The chapter encompasses about four and a half pages.

> I . . . felt indeed sure I had made a mistake.
> The little girl . . . affected me on the spot . . .
> . . . as I almost felt it . . .
> I felt within half an hour . . .
> . . . a sound or two . . . that I had fancied I heard.
> But these fancies were not marked enough . . .

> I felt quite sure she would presently . . .
> I remember feeling the impulse . . .
> What I felt the next day . . .
> I had the fancy of being . . .

Nor do the clues cease after the first chapter. They abound literally from first to last. These excerpts come from the final chapter.

> I felt how voluntarily . . . I *might.*
> I could feel in the sudden fever . . .
> I felt that the cause was mine . . .
> I felt myself . . .
> The only thing he felt was . . .
> I seemed to float not into clearness . . .
> . . . which . . . I suffered, feeling . . .
> I felt a sick swim . . .
> . . . it now, to my sense, filled the room . . .
> at the end of a minute I began to feel . . .

So there we have it. We trust that none will argue that the repetitions are fortuitous or careless. The admirers of James's artistry as a prose stylist would find such an argument hard to bear. On the contrary, we fancy or feel—nay, are convinced—that James sounded these recurring notes purposefully and artfully to establish the tone of "*felt*" trouble for which he was striving.

～～～～～～～～～～～～～～～～～～～～～～～～～～～～～～

III. *Approaches to the Tale and Its Heroine*

～～～～～～～～～～～～～～～～～～～～～～～～～～～～～～

R EAD HURRIEDLY (and it is difficult to read at any other pace), *The Turn of the Screw* has few peers for "dreadful—dreadfulness . . . general uncanny ugliness and horror and pain," to quote Douglas in the prologue. One has only to review the multitude of obviously sincere, frequently superlative expressions of terror indicated in the bibliography to suspect that as a horror story it has, not few, but no peers.

Is it not perverse, then, to subtract from the dreadfulness of this most gripping of all ghost stories by questioning the validity of its ghosts, by minimizing, denigrating, or banishing them altogether? Is this not replacing the "fairy-tale pure and simple," as James called it, with a dreary case history of some sort of hardly provable derangement? To tamper with those creatures Peter Quint and Miss Jessel, to attempt to rob the tale of their hideous presences, to *deprive* readers of them, so to speak—is this not to exercise the kind of meanness that prompts some leering adults to deprive children's imaginations of Santa Claus? Why not cast one's lot with the apparitionists and settle back to shudder at the tale as a ghost story, nothing more?

Because there is no settling back. After even a casual exposure to the nonapparitionist theory, with its distinguished and persuasive proponents, there is always the nagging suspicion that there must be something in it. If only there were some way to enjoy *The Turn of the Screw* from both points of view.

As a matter of fact, there is a way, and a very simple one. One of the present writers stumbled on it years ago. He read the novel when young and innocent of any knowledge of the nonapparitionists, abandoning himself totally to what Heywood Broun calls its "hideous thralldom." A decade later he read Edmund Wilson's "The Ambiguity of Henry James." With this essay in mind he reread the tale forthwith. He was thus able over a period of years to enjoy it on at least two levels—one starring a noble, courageous governess, the other a demented governess in a setting adorned with Freudian womb and phallic symbols—all the trappings.

He next made an effort to share this ideal approach with three classes of bright freshmen. The effort succeeded handsomely, with the aid of *Five Kinds of Writing,* containing both the story and Wilson's article. Though unable to offer his classes the leisurely, decade-long schedule he himself enjoyed, the instructor assigned first the story, then Edmund Wilson, then the story again, then an essay to be written on the topic "What Happens in *The Turn of the Screw*" from the point of view of either the children or Mrs. Grose.

The three classes contained that usual handful of enterprising, eager students who had purchased their textbooks, immediately scrutinized the table of contents, and already read the novel and Wilson's commentary on it so as to be that much ahead in their assignments. Or perhaps they read the not yet assigned story simply because they liked to read. Most of them enlisted proudly in the instructor's conspiracy, though doubtless a few in the eight-o'clock section passed the word about Wilson to their particular friends in the eleven-o'clock section, who in turn enlightened their cronies in the two-o'clock section. By far the larger number of them, however, raced horrified through the story, next pondered Wilson's hypothesis, and finally restudied the tale, feeling very scholarly no doubt. It is a tribute to James's text that no one seemed to tire of it. The themes were the best set the instructor had all year.

But no doubt there are others who are now ready to journey through the labyrinth at Bly. Torrential though the river of critical discussion of *The Turn of the Screw* has been, there is more, much more, to be said about the characters of the governess and Mrs. Grose, the relationship between the two women, the interplay between the governess and the children, and the action in the tale.

Before beginning to read the governess' manuscript, Douglas, its custodian for twenty years, supplies a few words of prologue that are "really required for a proper intelligence" of the narrative. In his speech Douglas seems calm, measured, judicious, trustworthy. What he tells us we are presumably to accept as true. He is, in short, the chorus character.

When he knew the governess, she was "a most charming person . . . the most agreeable woman I've ever known in her position; she'd have been worthy of any whatever." Apparitionists emphasize this "character reference." Nonapparitionists, on the other hand, would point out that Douglas knew her when she was about thirty and his younger sister's governess, while her stay at Bly had occurred long before, when she was twenty. What she had been doing during the ten years after she left Bly and before she joined the Douglas family he does not specify. Nonapparitionists might guess that she had passed the decade in a nursing home for the mentally deranged, repairing her shattered nerves and turning herself from a virtual lunatic into a most charming person.

At any rate, she had never told anyone her story. Even if one argues, with the apparitionists, that the demons which haunted her were sterling, bona-fide ghosts, how could her history recommend her to any future employer? Besides, what woman is willing to bare the details of a frustrating, one-sided love affair?

She was, Douglas goes on to say, "the youngest of several daughters of a poor country parson." These words provide an interesting if brief revelation of her background that might invite the attentive reader to all sorts of speculation. The youngest of several daughters. Was she doomed perpetually to wear clothes handed down from elder sisters? Did they bully or spoil her? Her father a poor country parson. Did she spend her girlhood in genteel poverty surrounded by the countrified and the narrow, by piety, by sanctimoniousness? Could her childhood have been not unlike Ernest Pontifex's? Either James aimlessly allowed Douglas to vouchsafe this account of her youth, or it will inevitably be reflected in her manuscript, in her behavior at Bly.

On many a page of her narrative the effect of her poverty is discernible. Her employer, as Douglas tells us, has impressed her "as rich, but as fearfully extravagant," his town house in Harley Street as "vast and imposing," and the salary he offers as much exceeding "her modest measure"; she is nevertheless unprepared for the grandeur of Bly, his country house. Arriving in a "commodious fly," she gapes at the greatness of Bly that makes it "a different affair from my own scant home." As Flora shows her around, what she sees strikes her as "the view of a castle of romance inhabited by a rosy sprite." The lake at Bly overwhelms her, though it may be "a sheet of water less remarkable than" it at first appears to her "untravelled eyes," her "acquaintance with sheets of water" being small.

She describes her new quarters in fulsome detail—the "large, impressive room, one of the best in the house, the great state bed . . . the figured full draperies, the long glasses" in which, for the first time, she can see herself from head to foot. As she savors the baronial appointments, one guesses that the draperies at the scant parsonage were neither full nor figured and that she shared a bed with one of her several sisters, with whom she took turns at the mirror. And now a sumptuous room of her own, with chevals.

Soon she habitually walks in the grounds and enjoys, "almost with a sense of property" that amuses and flatters her, "the beauty and dignity of the place." What is more, after a constitutional she may sit at supper with four tall candles. It is all quite enough to dazzle a poor country girl. What a pity that she must occasionally be wrenched back to reality by some reminder of her poverty: the pair of gloves, for example, that have "required three stitches and . . . received them—with a publicity perhaps not edifying." Ah, the mortification of having to betray one's poverty, publicly, with a pair of ragged gloves!

The novel luxuries which she carefully notes are not always material. She learns something that has "not been one of the teachings of my small smothered life": to be amused and amusing. The children display "a delightful endless appetite for passages in my own history," to which she treats them repeatedly. But when the passages come, how revealing of the pitiful circumscription of her life they are. The children learn "everything that had ever happened to me. . . . the story of my smallest adventures and of those of my brothers and sisters and of the cat and the dog at home . . . of the furniture and arrangement of our house, and of the conversation of the old women of our village," including "Goody Gosling's celebrated *mot.*" As a climax to these memoirs she lists "the cleverness of the vicarage pony." It is enough to make one weep. With the children she has for the first time "known space and air and freedom . . . and consideration," and consideration she finds sweet.

Some index to how narrow an intellectual climate she has grown up in, back in Hampshire, is provided by her reading habits at her new post. She avails herself of "a roomful of old books at Bly" and sits up reading Fielding's *Amelia* till dawn. Eighteenth-century fiction, we learn, "appealed to the unavowed curiosity of my youth." Yet not "so much as . . . a stray specimen" had ever penetrated her "sequestered home." At the hands of the parson the eighteenth-century novelists suffered "a distinctly deprecated renown" and no admittance. How his deprecations must have piqued his daughter's curiosity. To have to wait for an entire short lifetime, in a house that probably admitted only collected sermons and ecclesiastical periodicals, to satisfy that curiosity— pathetic. She has still longer to wait, incidentally, before she can satisfy her curiosity about the drama, if one may judge by her likening the first apparition to an actor, then confessing, "I've never seen one, but so I suppose them."

Her occasional comments about her father make one wish for more. Along with the tales of Goody Gosling and the vicarage pony she in-

forms the children of "many particulars of the whimsical bent of my
father." The "whimsical bent" is a result of James's revisions for the
edition of 1908, his substitution for the reading of 1898—"eccentric
nature." The latter encouraged Harold C. Goddard to surmise that the
parson "is of a psychically unbalanced nature; he may, indeed, even
have been insane." Believing the governess to be demented also, Goddard asserts that her manuscript clarifies certain of the causes of her
insanity. The "hereditary seed of the disease . . . is hinted at in the one
reference to the young woman's father." Goddard's hypotheses do not
attract universal agreement, but everyone must agree that being reared
by such a poor country parson—whether given to eccentricities or to
whims—could have done little to stabilize his daughter's psyche.

However that may be, the governess comes to depend on the charm
of her pupils as "an antidote to any pain," and she suffers "more pains
than one," including "disturbing letters from home, where things were
not going well." What things? Family finances? Are those left at home
being subjected to unusual severities from a whimsical father who bans
as sinful Richardson and most certainly Fielding, Smollett, and Sterne?
Given free rein, the imagination conjures up all sorts of questions and
answers. For example, does the Hampshire parson deserve to be mentioned in the same breath with Edward Moulton-Barret or another
Jamesian domestic tyrant, Dr. Sloper of Washington Square?

There may be a reflection of the parson in the governess' attitude toward males in general. Seeing Miles decked out in his Sunday clothes,
she meditates on his "whole title to independence, the rights of his sex
and situation." As for his relationship to his little sister, the governess
marvels that there is "a little boy in the world who could have for the
inferior age, sex and intelligence so fine a consideration." And is not
the following curious remark ultimately also a commentary on her
father: "the way in which a man pays his highest tribute to a woman is
apt to be but by the more festal celebration of one of the sacred laws of
his comfort"?

Finally, one would give much to know to what extent the governess
is indebted to her father, whose business it is to castigate sin, for her

habit of thinking the worst of certain characters, alive and dead, whom she meets in the course of the action. To understand all is to forgive all, and in the opinion of many the governess desperately needs forgiveness before her tale is told—largely for ascribing wickedness to those who are not provably wicked. *Honi soit qui mal y pense.*

IV. *Effusiveness and Instability*

THE GOVERNESS has certain other pronounced characteristics that merit attention. Though Douglas makes no mention of them, they too seem the result of her childhood in a large family where a whimsical father was perhaps stern rather than affectionate and where the competition for whatever affection was dispensed may have been keen. At any rate, the parson's youngest daughter betrays on almost every page her urgent, pathetic need to love and be loved. Her need manifests itself in both the way she writes and speaks and the way she acts.

No alert reader of her manuscript can fail to be struck by her lavish use of superlatives, by the astonishing effusiveness of her language. She is—I am afraid it is really the only word for her—gushy, to a degree. Let each reader marvel in his own private discovery of the extent of her gushiness. A handful of illustrations will suffice here.

Upon first meeting Miles, she pronounces him "incredibly beautiful" and takes "him to my heart for . . . something divine." She envisages her pupils as "a pair of little grandees, of princes of the blood." Flora is "the most beautiful child" she has ever seen; she can feel "no uneasiness in a connexion with anything so beatific as the radiant image

of my little girl," yet "the vision" of Flora's "angelic beauty" so un-
does her that the night after their first meeting she cannot sleep. There
are enough of such rhapsodies to put one in mind of the less restrained
Elizabethan sonneteers, of Petrarch on Laura, of Dante on Beatrice.

The lack of moderation in her diction is exceeded only by her sometimes frantic physical demonstrations of affection—if affection is the
right word. In one scene, catching Flora in her arms, the governess
covers her with kisses in which there is "a sob of atonement." She
"grips" Flora "with a spasm that, wonderfully," the child submits to
"without a cry or a sign of fright." Both children are "perpetually
bowed over and hugged." There are moments when "I knew myself to
catch them up by an irresistible impulse and press them to my heart."

Even having gone to bed and presumably to sleep does not insure the
children against her displays of love. After Miles has retired, she comes
to his bedside, places "on his small shoulders hands of . . . tenderness,"
kisses him, and has to make, while she folds him for a minute in her
arms, the most stupendous effort not to cry. The incident closes "after
another embrace." In another bedroom scene with the poor boy she
drops on her knees beside his bed, holds his hand, throws herself "upon
him and in the tenderness of my pity" embraces him. In the final episode of the novel, however, she reaches truly frenzied heights. She
"gets hold" of Miles, draws him close, "enfolds" him "with a moan of
joy," draws him close again, holds him to her breast, kisses his forehead, shakes him—"but . . . for pure tenderness," springs "straight
upon him," tries to "press him against me." In the next to the last
sentence of the book she holds him, "it may be imagined with what a
passion."

Mrs. Grose is the beneficiary not only of the governess' affection but
of her confidences as well, and the two women's séances are often as
fraught with desperate action as the scenes between the governess and
the children. The governess embraces and kisses Mrs. Grose, throws
herself into Mrs. Grose's arms, falls on Mrs. Grose's breast with lam-
entations overflowing. One is not surprised to read in one place that
Mrs. Grose is evidently seeking to avoid the governess, who neverthe-

less finds the poor woman and "detains" her, "holding her there with a hand on her arm," and a few sentences later holds her tighter. Again she puts out her hand to Mrs. Grose, holds her "hard a little," and feels "a kind of support in the shy heave of her surprise."

The governess is continually busy with her detaining hand. She is a grabber as well as a gusher. Had her manuscript been published last week, it could scarcely have escaped attention in that irreverent column of *The New Yorker* entitled "Infatuation with the Sound of One's Own Words Department." The very column, greatly abridged, might read something like this: "I seized my colleague's arm" (p. 527); "I could only grasp her more quickly" (p. 528); "I continued, seizing my colleague" (p. 528); "I seized her almost with joy" (p. 536). To be confided in or doted on by the governess is a smothering, not to say bruising, experience.

Verbal and physical outbursts of the kind just examined—and scores of additional passages could be cited—provided the basis for certain critical opinions of John Lydenberg and Osborn Andreas. The former, describing the governess' relationship to her charges, notices how she "well-nigh smothers them in demonstrations. . . . These caresses are not expressions of a spontaneous, relaxed affection." Andreas also remarks the governess' "jealous, clutching love for the children," her "emotional cannibalism."

So she was the youngest of several daughters of a poor country parson. This and other information that Douglas gives in the prologue cannot be taken lightly, one realizes after observing how interestingly the implications of Douglas's statement are developed in the governess' own narrative. Having just undertaken a partial review of her character, we recall with sympathy James's resentment of the critic who objected that he had not sufficiently characterized the governess, neglecting to endow her with "signs and marks, features and humours."

Even so, in Glenn A. Reed's opinion, her character "is not sufficiently particularized to hold the spotlight," while Lyon N. Richardson surmises that "James merely used the governess as the center of revelation, not as the center of the story as well." Carl Van Doren also argues that James "desired her to serve solely as the lens through which the action could be seen, without refraction or coloring. . . . the narrator must be lost sight of in the narration."

In the light of the passages we have noted, we cannot agree with these critical opinions. Nor can we accept unreservedly James's remark that he kept the governess "impersonal save for the most obvious and indispensable little note of neatness, firmness and courage." To a good many readers, including the authors of this study, the impoverished, effusive, love-starved young gentlewoman with her ragged gloves, full-length mirrors, grand airs, and hugs and kisses is all too real a person.

The first few pages of her narrative validate still other information which Douglas gives in his preamble. He describes her as "a fluttered anxious girl out of a Hampshire vicarage" who regards the prospect of her new position "as slightly grim." After accepting the job, she suffers "a couple of very bad days" during which life, for her, is "a succession of flights and drops, a little see-saw of the right throbs and the wrong." Is this not a state verging on what the learned in such matters call manic-depressive?

Whatever the proper term may be, it is a state that James evidently wanted to make conspicuous as he dictated the version of 1898 and still more conspicuous as he revised this text for the edition of 1908. On the very first page of the governess' narrative she confesses, in 1898, that as she drove through the summer countryside toward Bly "my fortitude mounted afresh and, as we turned into the avenue, encountered a reprieve that was probably but a proof of the point to which it had sunk." The "mounted afresh" and "had sunk" develop the theme of "a succession of flights and drops" introduced in the governess' first sentence, but not as pointedly as in the 1908 version, where "my fortitude revived and, as we turned into the avenue, took a flight that was probably but a proof of the point to which it had sunk."

Also enroute to Bly, "in the coach, I fear I had rather brooded." After arriving, "I slept little that night—I was too much excited." Restlessness forces her several times to "rise and wander about my room," to watch the dawn, and to listen "for the possible recurrence of a sound or two . . . that I had fancied I heard. . . . But these fancies were not marked enough not to be thrown off." The next day she has, not exactly "a reaction from the cheer of my arrival," but "only a slight oppression," a "drop," induced by a realization of her large responsibilities. Contemplating these makes her, "freshly, a little scared"; "in this agitation" she delays beginning lessons with Flora.

The see-saw takes a real dip, however, at the end of her first full day at Bly, which winds up in keen apprehension, brought on by "an incident that . . . had deeply disconcerted me." The incident turns out to be a letter from her employer enclosing another letter, from the headmaster of Miles's school, and directing her to deal with the matter. We can assay the weight of her apprehension from her odd treatment of these communications. She puts off opening the headmasters's "a long time," breaks its seal "with a great effort," takes it, seal broken but still unread, to her room, and attacks it "only just before going to bed." It costs her "a second sleepless night." The next day, not surprisingly, she is "full of distress," which finally gets "so the better" of her that she decides to talk the matter over with Mrs. Grose.

So much for the state of her nerves at the end of the first paragraph of Chapter II—that is, at the end of the first five printed pages of her 108-page narrative. Her first experience with an apparition—or hallucination, as nonapparitionists would have it—does not occur until the middle of Chapter III. For our study of her instability of nerves and sleeplessness we have scrupulously drawn upon only this early part of her manuscript in order to demonstrate to apparitionists and nonapparitionists alike that she is nervously unstrung even before the hideous aggravation of the apparitions overtakes her. Thus early in the story her condition is not ideal for coping with apparitions. Nonapparitionists would put it another way: she is sufficiently sleepless and nervously overwrought to invite hallucinations.

After the revelations of her first five pages, what is one to make of certain apparitionist estimates of the governess' character? To quote three, Robert Liddell sees it as very carefully established in the prologue and maintained throughout the story as that of "a girl keeping her balance and courage in the most frightful circumstances." According to Glenn A. Reed, James presents her "as a charming person of good breeding with no obvious signs of mental instability either before or after the events of the story." And Oliver Evans detects strong "evidence of the governess' stability of personality." To say so is to mistake a see-saw for the Rock of Gibraltar.

v. *The Very Coinage of the Brain?*

O F THE thousands of words expended upon the supernatural and the psychological at Bly, Leon Edel's in *The Ghostly Tales* impress us as the most cogent. In Edel's opinion these tales are not ghost stories in the conventional sense, but treat only haunted characters— those haunted by phantoms usually of their own creation. Of paramount interest to James are the folk who see the ghosts. Fear and "persons who are victims of *unconscious obsession* (and Henry James used these words before the modern era of psychiatry)—these are the subjects of most of the ghostly tales." As for James's own remarks about Quint and Miss Jessel in his preface, they are "not 'ghosts' at all, as we now know the ghost, but goblins, elves, imps and demons as loosely constructed as those of the old trials for witchcraft."

Edel believes that James intended to make *The Turn of the Screw* "the record of the young governess' mind, as he did with other[s] of his characters in his ghostly tales." James skillfully and imaginatively depicted these characters, "made them creatures of flesh and blood, giving us the manifest content of their minds so that a psychiatric 'diagnosis' can be validly attempted." As a matter of fact, Edel continues,

The Turn of the Screw can be studied on three levels: "as a ghostly tale, pure and simple"; "as a deeply fascinating psychological 'case'—which is what those interested in applying psychiatry to the tale have done"; and "as a projection of Henry James's own haunted state."

The second approach to the story we now propose esentially to adopt throughout the rest of this study. In our opinion James's masterpiece is a richer, more subtle, and more horrifying tale according to the non-apparitionist reading than it is from the apparitionist point of view. We agree with the late Wolcott Gibbs, who found the nonapparitionist reading "more tenable than any supernatural hypothesis and also a good deal more shocking, maniacs being, to my taste, considerably more disturbing than ghosts."

Before proceeding, however, we want to make two things clear. First, we do not pretend to special knowledge of psychiatry in general or of the Freudian in particular. Second, even if we could claim expertness in these matters, we should persist in regarding *The Turn of the Screw* as primarily a work of art. It is just that, for us, James's magnificent art in this story is inseparable from his subtle treatment of the governess' devious, probably diseased, and certainly terrifying mental processes. Perhaps all that need be said about this was said some years ago on the radio program *New Invitation to Learning* when Allen Tate, discussing *The Turn of the Screw* with Katherine Anne Porter and Mark Van Doren, asserted, "James knew substantially all that Freud knew before Freud came on the scene"; and Miss Porter added, "All major artists do." Freud himself wrote, "Imaginative writers are valuable colleagues [of the psychoanalyst], and their testimony is to be rated very highly, because they have a way of knowing many of the things between heaven and earth which are not dreamed of in our philosophy."

Not that it is safe to overlook whatever technical psychological lore James may have commanded personally and turned to good artistic account. Edel wisely insists on making allowances for James's familiarity with the psychological knowledge of his time, with Charcot's work, and with his brother William's investigations, not to mention his own experience with what he called an "immense hallucination." Oscar

Cargill's review of the late-nineteenth-century Freud led him to argue strongly that one of the novel's "public sources" (as opposed to the "private source"—Archbishop Benson's anecdote—which James acknowledges in his notebooks) was "The Case of Miss Lucy R." in the *Studien über Hysterie* (1895) of Breuer and Freud. The parallels between the experiences of Miss Lucy and James's governess strike some as impressive, illuminating, all but conclusive. Others dismiss them as incomplete and irrelevant—such is the irreconcilability of apparitionists and nonapparitionists—and judge Cargill's position untenable.

It is not out of the question, however, that a systematic exploration of psychological studies available to James before 1898 will uncover still other material which nonapparitionists will find suggestive. Here, for example, is another treatise, happened upon in the most casual and random of searches: *Hallucinations and Illusions* (London, W. Scott, 1897), by Edmund Parish. This author discusses the conditions, causes, and victims of hallucinations in terms that startlingly recall certain conditions, causes, actions, and mental processes at Bly. His book deserves reviewing as possibly a second "outside source" of *The Turn of the Screw*.

There are several reasons, apart from those advanced by Edel, why James could have interested himself in such a work. As Cargill says, James inevitably gained a personal, sometimes intimate knowledge of his sister Alice's mental illness with its attendant delusions and fantasies. His interest in these could scarcely have expired with her death in 1892. Also, Parish was a disciple of the pioneer student of such matters, William James, whom he often quotes. Then what of the title, place, and date of publication—*Hallucinations and Illusions*, London, 1897? Though *The Turn of the Screw* first appeared in weekly installments in *Collier's* from January 27 to April 16, 1898, James began dictating the story in the fall of 1897 and on December 1 wrote Mrs. William James that he had finished it.

What if Edel and the nonapparitionists are right and James intended at the outset to treat the involutions of the governess' diseased mind, hallucinations and all? Parish's book, the last word on the subject, was

conveniently at hand, fresh from the press. That James prepared himself for his task by studying Parish is not really susceptible of proof, of
course. Yet the treatise is interesting, to say the least, because in time,
in place, and (according to nonapparitionists) in subject matter it co-
incides exactly with *The Turn of the Screw*. In 1897 it was the latest
sober, scientific treatment of what many regard as James's central
theme. Here are some of Parish's details.

He states that hallucinations most frequently attack women fifteen to
thirty years of age, who experience more than half of all such seizures
during this period, and that the lustrum from twenty to twenty-five
yields the highest percentage of all. James's governess is twenty. (Alice
James's first violent attacks of hysteria occurred, incidentally, when she
was nearing twenty.) Parish's investigation of the causes of hallucinations also turns one's thoughts toward Bly. He lists 1) morbid emotional states, 2) a state of mental or physical exhaustion, 3) vivid
expectation, and 4) the hypnogenic tendency of prolonged reading. Let
us begin with the second and fourth causes.

After agreeing to take the position at Bly, the governess confesses
to suffering "a couple of very bad days." She says nothing of her nights
—until she actually assumes her duties; then she says plenty. She arrives, agitatedly, in the afternoon, and—"I slept little that night—I was
too much excited." Uneasiness makes her "several times rise and wander about my room," at last "to watch from my open window the faint
summer dawn." On her second day the letter from Miles's headmaster
comes to disturb her inordinately. Already her behavior seems peculiar,
to say the least. Would a good, sound sleep on her first night have rendered it less so?

To return to the headmaster's letter, "I had better have let it wait till
morning, for it gave me a second sleepless night." The next day she is
"full of distress," due partly no doubt to what Parish describes as a
state of mental or physical exhaustion. At this same early stage of her
narrative there are also copious indications of a morbid emotional state.
The two states, mutually aggravating, often operate simultaneously.

The brief quotations above, drawn from the two earliest chapters and the first six pages of the governess' recital, establish the fact that she was exhausted before Quint and Miss Jessel began haunting her. If Dr. Parish had been studying her behavior, he could have ticked off one of the causes on his list. Whether the apparitions, once they start appearing to her, improve her repose may be imagined. Like Macbeth, she seems at times totally to lack the season of all natures, sleep. After Quint's second visitation she gives herself over to an hour of nervous prostration and next to a hysterical conference with Mrs. Grose that lasts till after midnight; still, "in the immediate later hours in especial —for it may be imagined whether I slept"—she agonizes, sleepless.

After the third visitation (this one from Miss Jessel, the governess believes), she and Mrs. Grose have another of their grisly conferences "in the small hours," while the house sleeps. The house, but not the conferees, who are still at it when "the grey dawn admonished us to separate." The fourth visitation, from Quint again, on the stairs, robs the governess of sleep for who knows how many nights. For the moment, we can only quote the governess on "the general complexion . . . of my nights" after meeting Quint on the stairs. She repeatedly sits up till she doesn't know when; instead of wooing sleep she takes turns in the hallway; and according to our calculations she gets little or no sleep for *ten nights straight running*. On the eleventh, "weary with vigils," she feels that she may "again without laxity lay myself down at my old hour." Needless to say, she goes to sleep immediately—only to sit straight up about one in the morning. Awake, sleepless again.

Whether following Parish's lead or not, James makes so considerable a point of her sleeplessness that the wonder is she stays on her feet at all. After habitual, prolonged insomnia how could any twenty-year-old avoid a state of utter physical exhaustion? The apparitionist who would attribute this solely to a natural, understandable reaction to ghostly visitants and to her heroic vigilance should remind himself that James indicates the pattern of her sleeplessness—the general complexion of her nights, as she calls it—*before* she encounters any apparitions at all.

As for the hypnogenic tendency of prolonged reading, the fourth cause of hallucinations in Parish, the governess' hunger for literature and how it remained unappeased in the Hampshire vicarage has already received mention. At Bly feasting replaces famine. According to an extended but gripping passage in Chapter IX,

I had not gone to bed; I sat reading by a couple of candles. There was a roomful of old books at Bly—last-century fiction some of it. . . . I remember that the book I had in my hand was Fielding's "Amelia"; also that I was wholly awake. I recall further both a general conviction that it was horribly late and a particular objection to looking at my watch . . . I recollect in short that though I was deeply interested in my author I found myself, at the turn of a page and with his spell all scattered, looking straight up from him and hard at the door of my room. . . . Then, with all the marks of a deliberation that must have seemed magnificent had there been anyone to admire it, I laid down my book, rose to my feet and, taking a candle, went straight out of the room and, from the passage, on which my light made little impression, noiselessly closed and locked the door.

I can say now neither what determined nor what guided me, but I went straight along the lobby, holding my candle high, till I came within sight of the tall window that presided over the great turn of the staircase. At this point I precipitately found myself aware of three things. They were practically simultaneous, yet they had flashes of succession. My candle, under a bold flourish, went out, and I perceived, by the uncovered window, that the yielding dusk of earliest morning rendered it unnecessary. Without it, the next instant, I knew that there was a figure on the stair. I speak of sequences, but I required no lapse of seconds to stiffen myself for a third encounter with Quint. The apparition had reached the landing halfway up and was therefore on the spot nearest the window, where, at sight of me, it stopped short and fixed me exactly as it had fixed me from the tower and from the garden. He knew me as well as I knew him; and so, in the cold faint twilight, with a glimmer in the high glass and another on the polish of the oak stair below, we faced each other in our common intensity. He was absolutely, on this occasion, a living detestable dangerous presence.

In this scene could Parish have detected two of the causes of hallucinations on his list, the hypnogenic tendency of prolonged reading and physical exhaustion (she has read through the night and slept not at all), and consequently diagnosed her case as typical? Despite her recollection that she was wholly awake, lovers of opera will associate some of the details in the episode with certain exquisite though tense musical moments. The governess' magnificent deliberation, her noiseless gliding, the candle (held high and boldly flourished), the great turn of the staircase—ah yes, the climactic scenes in *Lucia di Lammermoor* and *La Sonambula*; even *I Puritani* and Ambroise Thomas's *Hamlet*, with Ophelia's mad scene; Maria Callas as Lucia, all in white, descending the stairs, or as Verdi's Lady Macbeth, light and all, and again the great staircase. If in the future a nonapparitionist composer should follow Benjamin Britten's example in making *The Turn of the Screw* into an opera, he ought to try his hand at setting this scene. It is in the grand tradition.

Since fastening the eyes upon the printed page for extended periods qualifies an exhausted reader for hallucinations, what of the governess' other concentrated use of the eyes that appears to be connected with her seeing Quint and Miss Jessel? Before two of the major visitations she is busily engaged with her needles, knitting or otherwise. In the next to the last chapter, during her final interview with Miles, "I had always my hypocrisy of 'work,' behind which I now gained the sofa. Steadying myself with it there as I had repeatedly done at those moments of torment that I have described as the moments of my knowing the children to be given to something from which I was barred, I sufficiently obeyed my habit of being prepared for the worst." As the tension of the scene inexorably rises, "I achieved thoughtfully a few loops of my knitting," and "oh my work preoccupied me"—just before leaping up and upon Miles and facing again what she imagines to be the ghost of Quint. Notice especially that applying herself to her knitting, sewing, or what not, is habitual during certain "moments of torment."

At tea time, before seeing Quint for the second time (Chapter IV), she has also been doing a bit of sewing—mending her gloves, to be exact. The most marked connection between sewing and seeing ghosts comes, however, when she fancies that Miss Jessel visits her and Flora beside the lake in Chapter VI.

Suddenly . . . I became aware that on the other side of the Sea of Azof [the lake at Bly] we had an interested spectator. The way this knowledge gathered in me was the strangest thing in the world. . . . I had sat down with a piece of work . . . on the old stone bench which overlooked the pond; and in this position I began to take in with certitude and yet without direct vision the presence, a good way off, of a third person. . . . There was no ambiguity in anything; none whatever at least in the conviction I from one moment to another found myself forming as to what I should see straight before me and across the lake as a consequence of raising my eyes. They were attached at this juncture to the stitching in which I was engaged. . . . Then I again shifted my eyes—I faced what I had to face.

The eeriness of this recital is enough to make girls—even sound sleepers and the thoroughly well adjusted—swear off excessive stitching, mending, embroidering, knitting, crocheting, tatting, and quilting forever, in the fear that these might propel one into the gehenna where evil spirits stalk, where even without looking one may take them in with certitude. Though it is of course for specialists in hypnogenesis to say authoritatively, once and for all, whether the governess' focusing her eyes upon her work, like her avid reading, constitutes a further habitual prelude to hallucinations.

VI. *The Beauty of Her Passion*

THE CONDITION of the governess' nerves and her repose are not improved by the state of her heart. Long before assuming her responsibilities at Bly, long before she is beset by what she construes as ghostly
prowlers, the young, untried, nervous Hampshire girl fell in love. In
the prologue Douglas, again transmitting the governess' oral report to
him, characterizes her employer as "a bachelor in the prime of life . . .
handsome and bold and pleasant, off-hand and gay and kind. He struck
her, inevitably, as gallant and splendid. . . . She figured him as rich, but
as fearfully extravagant—saw him all in a glow of high fashion, of
good looks, of expensive habits, of charming ways with women." Naturally this dashing figure is never far from the fluttered girl's thoughts.

In delivering this and other requisite information, Douglas relies on
a special rapport with one member of his audience, the narrator of the
prologue. When an effusive lady auditor interrupts Douglas, "He took
no notice of her; he looked at me," the narrator writes. "It was to me in
particular that he appeared to propound this—appeared almost to appeal for aid not to hesitate" in sending for the governess' manuscript.
Why she had never related her story before, "You'll easily judge,"

Douglas declares; "*you* will." The sensitive, sophisticated narrator does not disappoint him. "I fixed him too. 'I see. She was in love'." Douglas laughs for the first time and replies, "You *are* acute. Yes, she was in love," though her manuscript "*won't* tell . . . in any literal vulgar way" the history of her love.

The prologue, however, leaves no one in doubt. When she accepts the offer of the bachelor and when "for a moment, disburdened, de-lighted, he held her hand, thanking her for the sacrifice, she already felt rewarded." She had succumbed to "the seduction exercised by the splendid young man," the narrator suggests. "She saw him only twice" is Douglas's rejoinder. "Yes, but that's just the beauty of her passion," the narrator says; and Douglas agrees, "It *was* the beauty of it."

A strong word, "passion." Nothing could be clearer than that James's chorus character, Douglas, considers the governess' manuscript not merely a horror story, but a horror story complicated by the pas-sion of the teller of the tale and, some think, the principal character in it. Douglas and the perspicacious narrator of the prologue make so much of this passion that to lose its impact on the governess' character may be to lose one of the main points of the novel, to remove one's self from the honorable, acute company of Douglas and the narrator, and to join the company of James's obtuse critic who complained that the gov-erness wanted characterization. Let us therefore turn again to the very early pages of the governess' own account and look there for signs of the passion which afflicts her.

In the second sentence of her manuscript she speaks of "rising . . . to meet his appeal." Upon first seeing Bly, which is a far grander estate than she had imagined, she thinks "the proprietor still more of a gentle-man," apparently for not expatiating on the grandeur of his country house. His gentlemanly reticence suggests that she may be on the point of enjoying "a matter beyond his promises." She finds Flora so beau-tiful that she wonders "why my employer hadn't made more of a point to me of this."

Mrs. Grose says that if Flora seems lovely to her new governess, then she *will* be smitten by Miles; the governess replies, "Well, that, I think, is what I came for—to be carried away. I'm afraid, however . . . I'm rather easily carried away. I was carried away in London! . . . In Harley Street."

Mrs. Grose's next remark, "Well, Miss, you're not the first—and you won't be the last," probably affords scant comfort to the love-stricken girl, who nevertheless "could laugh" and reply, "Oh I've no pretension . . . to being the only one." Less of a laughing matter is the letter she receives "in the hand of my employer." It is "composed but of a few words," she carefully records, and these few are businesslike, nothing more. Throughout the rest of the novel she has not another syllable from him, nor does she see him again, ever.

Yet her passion does not expire in the face of his silence. It lives, it grows. Soon she is "lifted aloft on the great wave of infatuation [for her employer] and pity [for the children]." In her first weeks at Bly the infatuated girl enjoys "my own hour" in the late afternoon when the children have been put to bed. She strolls about the grounds feeling calm and self-righteous, congratulating herself on her common sense, discretion, and propriety, virtues sure to please her employer—if he should ever notice them. Fulfilling his commission gives her great joy. She comforts herself with the faith that her efficiency and excellent de-portment will some day come to his attention.

One of the thoughts that, as I don't in the least shrink now from noting, used to be with me in these wanderings was that it would be as charming as a charming story suddenly to meet some one. Some one would appear there at the turn of a path and would stand before me and smile and ap-prove. I didn't ask more than that—I only asked that he should *know*; and the only way to be sure he knew would be to see it, and the kind light of it, in his handsome face. That was exactly present to me—by which I mean the face was—when, on the first of these occasions, at the end of a long June day, I stopped short. . . . What arrested me on the spot—and with a shock much greater than any vision had allowed for—was the sense that my imagination had, in a flash, turned real. He did stand there!—but high up, beyond the lawn and at the very top of the tower . . . yet it was not at such an elevation that the figure I had so often thus invoked seemed most in place.

It produced in me, this figure, in the clear twilight, I remember, two distinct gasps of emotion, which were, sharply, the shock of my first and that of my second surprise. My second was a violent perception of the mistake of my first: the man who met my eyes was not the person I had precipitately supposed . . . and the figure that faced me was . . . as little anyone else I knew as it was the image that had been in my mind. I had not seen it in Harley Street.

This arresting passage has required quoting at some length because no paraphrase or bald synopsis could possibly convey the extent and profundity of the governess' emotional involvement so devastatingly as James's quiet, almost ruminative, yet intense prose. Here is passion indeed, to impel her "so often" to invoke her employer's figure, to wear his image in her mind. Only the image which appears on the tower is not that of her employer. How to explain this shocking departure from her hopes and expectations?

The apparitionist explanation is prompt and assured. The image is one of a pair of ghosts, Peter Quint and Miss Jessel, that infest Bly and appear to the governess time after time. As F. R. Leavis puts it, in "James's 'What Maisie Knew'," Quint, like Miss Jessel, is the consistently evil ghost of an evil man. The scene quoted above merely describes the first of the apparitions.

When the governess sees the same image the second time, she describes him to Mrs. Grose, who, Leavis goes on to say, "recognizes the dead valet in the highly specific description of the sinister intruder given by the governess." In the words of A. J. A. Waldock, this "identification is absolute. Mrs. Grose is not merely reminded of Peter Quint by the description: she recognizes him positively in it. The man the governess saw *was* Peter Quint, or his absolute double: this is a fact of the story." Few explanations could be more positive in tone than these.

Nonapparitionists are less positive of the image's identity, preferring to scrutinize the emotional climate in which it first appears. So the governess is arrested by "the sense that my imagination had, in a flash, turned real"? The nonapparitionist is not surprised. If ever a girl has, as they say, been "asking for it," the governess has. How she has longed for it, invited it, willed it. Here, to borrow the term from Edmund Parish's causes of hallucinations, is "vivid expectation" in full measure. The nonapparitionist shares her sense that her imagination has indeed turned real and argues that her experience with the image is a figment of that passion-tossed imagination; that it is highly subjective; that it is self-induced; that it is—to use a word which is on every tongue—psychosomatic.

Does she not simply provide another warning against the perils of loving not wisely but too well? Has not her passion for the bachelor of Harley Street driven her to depart from reality? Is not her compulsion to see "some one" so powerful that see him she does? Only the "some one" she has conjured up is not the one for whom she has longed.

If she is suffering the retribution that lies in wait for all who love baselessly and excessively, her shocking experience makes apparent an artful, exquisite irony in the interchange between Douglas and the narrator in the prologue (only the relevant conversation is quoted, in dialogue form):

Douglas. She saw him only twice.
Narrator. Yes, but that's just the beauty of her passion.
Douglas. It *was* the beauty of it.

Beauty indeed. The lengths to which her passion drives her are anything but beautiful. Its effects upon her have been traced only through Chapter III. But one could argue that upon this passion the major action of the whole novel is predicated. What is one to make, for instance, of a passage in Chapter XII, halfway through the governess' narrative of twenty-four chapters? Here, after many apparitions and endless expositions of her dreadful theories to Mrs. Grose, she seriously alarms the housekeeper by announcing that it is only a matter of time until Peter Quint and Miss Jessel destroy their compliant victims, unless "of course, we can prevent!" The governess has gone too far: the housekeeper now plays her trump card:

Mrs. Grose. Their uncle must do the preventing. He must take them away.
The Governess. And who's to make him?

Mrs. Grose. You, Miss.

The Governess. By writing to him that his house is poisoned and his little nephew and niece mad?

Mrs. Grose. But if they *are*, Miss?

The Governess. And if I am myself, you mean? That's charming news to be sent him by a person enjoying his confidence and whose prime undertaking was to give him no worry.

Mrs. Grose. Yes, he do hate worry. That was the great reason—

The Governess. Why those fiends took him in so long? No doubt, though his indifference must have been awful. As I'm not a fiend, at any rate, I shouldn't take him in.

Mrs. Grose. Make him at any rate come to you.

The Governess. To *me?* "Him"?

Mrs. Grose. He ought to *be* here—he ought to help.

The Governess. You see me asking him for a visit? If you should so lose your head as to appeal to him for me—

Mrs. Grose. Yes, Miss?

The Governess. I would leave, on the spot, both him and you.

She prefers his indifference, awful though it is, to the inevitable consequences of his learning her interpretation of her experiences. Suppose he could be converted to apparitionism himself, prepared to accept the governess' inductions unreservedly? What could he do after accepting them but remove the poor possessed children at once from haunted Bly, away from the windows, the tower, and the lake where demons lurk? If he were to adopt a nonapparitionist posture, unwilling to believe in the objectivity of the governess' demons, what then? He could only relieve Bly of her presence forthwith—and, if merciful, help her family in Hampshire to have her committed to an asylum.

The governess says not a word of any possible benefit to the children which avuncular intervention might bring. Her concern is all for what would become of *her* bargain with *him, her* relationship with *him, his* opinion of *her.* Her concern is intensely personal, romantic, feminine— and selfish. She believes that "as a woman reads another" Mrs. Grose can see what she sees in the way of consequences: "his derision, his amusement, his contempt for the breakdown of my resignation at being left alone and for the fine machinery I had set in motion to attract his attention to my slighted charms. She didn't know—no one knew—how proud I had been to serve him and to stick to our terms."

Her slighted charms. Hell hath indeed no fury. The key words are "slighted charms" and "proud." Could the governess, in a moment of remarkable clearsightedness, be furnishing the reader with the proper explanation of all that has been tormenting her, and through her, the others at Bly? No nonapparitionist could wish for a more telling summation of Peter Quint and Miss Jessel, their relationship to the girl who evokes them, and their genesis in her frustrated passion for her employer: "the fine machinery I had set in motion to attract his attention to my slighted charms." It is magnificently ironical that with these bitter reflections thrown so sarcastically into her narrative the governess supplies an explicit, all-important analysis of the method in her madness.

Katherine Anne Porter, in *New Invitation to Learning*, summed up this method as follows: "In her attempt to vindicate herself she's doing the whole thing really at the expense of the children—I have always believed for the sake of destroying them, of putting them out of the way in some manner or other in order to clear a road to the master . . . no force has ever acted through either a saint or an evil person that wasn't somehow directed to further the ends and the ambitions and the hopes of that person, which makes me feel that the instrument [the governess] is not altogether so innocent and so helpless . . . the governess had her positive motive—she was in love with the master." Miss Porter comes closer to the truth, in our view, than does C. H. Grabo in speaking of the governess' "innocent love-story."

Finally, to return for a moment to Edmund Parish, first on his list of the causes of hallucinations is "morbid emotional states." That the governess' state, thanks in large measure to her tenacious, unrequited passion, is dangerously, morbidly emotional throughout the novel is a point that needs no further underscoring. Hamlet was right to include the pangs of despised love among the major ills of mankind.

VII. *'Tis an Accustomed Action with Her*

NONAPPARITIONIST readers disapprove of several expressions that habitually turn up in criticisms of *The Turn of the Screw*—for example, "visitations," "apparitions," "revenants," "evil spirits," "ghostly visitants," and the like. But what the governess suffers is so complicated that "hallucinations" also seems too simple. Maybe the juster word would be "seizures." These are no easier to describe—or always to detect—than the precise chronology of the story. An attempt to do so may be useful. Here are the readily detectable ones:

Seizure 1: Quint on the tower (Chapter III)
Seizure 2: Quint at the window (Chapter IV)
Seizure 3: Miss Jessel at the lake (Chapter VI)
Seizure 4: Quint on the stairs (Chapter IX)
Seizure 5: Miss Jessel on the stairs (Chapter X)
Seizure 6: Miss Jessel in the schoolroom (Chapter XV)
Seizure 7: Miss Jessel at the lake again (Chapter XX)
Seizure 8: Quint at the window again (Chapter XXIV)

This list comprises only those scenes in which the governess believes she sees Quint or Miss Jessel, and she sees them four times each, with admirable impartiality. Certain other episodes meriting discussion will receive it shortly. As for the eight above, an objective, dispassionate scrutiny of them—difficult because the governess' racing, eloquent account is apt to stifle objectivity—yields several meaningful recurrences. These could be of use even to diagnosticians alert to record symptoms, catatonic or otherwise, though critics sensitive to James's marvelous art may prefer to call them recurrent motifs or themes.

Most, but not all, of the seizures transpire when the light is less than perfect. To put it another way, the lighting effects are often ideal for "seeing things." Seizure 1 occurs late in the afternoon, "in the clear twilight"; and at "this same hour," the governess informs Mrs. Grose, the second seizure overtakes its victim, when "the afternoon light still lingered" on a rainy Sunday. The time of the fourth and fifth seizures can be identified as late, very late, in the course of sleepless nights. The former is illuminated partly by candle, partly by "the yielding dusk of earliest morning," or "the cold faint twilight [of dawn], with a glimmer in the high glass [of the window on the staircase landing] and another on the polish of the oak stair below."

Twilight, dusk, flickering candles, with attendant shadows no doubt, the palely glimmering dawn light, with reflections on polished oak— the most accomplished designer of lighting for the stage assigned to prepare a horror piece could learn much from James. One cannot swear that these crepuscular effects have a direct bearing on four of the governess' seizures. But they are splendid accompaniments, and certainly they could not have improved her normal vision despite her insistence, in writing about Seizure 1, that while it is in progress she sees everything "with a stranger sharpness," and about Seizure 2 that "my vision was instantaneous" as Quint appears "with I won't say greater distinctness, for that was impossible, but with a nearness that represented a forward stride in our intercourse." All this in the gloaming: she is lynx-eyed indeed. Or should one rather recall the poet's line about objects which flash upon the inward eye?

Discussing hallucinations in his *Principles of Psychology*, William James says of one case, "I can give no information as to the length of time occupied by this episode," an admission which Henry James almost seems to have in mind as the governess writes of her first seizure, "The great question, or one of these, is afterwards, I know, with regard to certain matters, the question of how long they have lasted. Well, this matter of mine, think what you will of it, lasted while I caught at a dozen possibilities."

The duration of her seizures concerns her more than once. Beset by Quint a second time, she says at first that he remains "but a few seconds"; then she gives him time to reappear, "but how long was it? I can't speak to the purpose today of the duration of these things. That kind of measure must have left me: they couldn't have lasted as they actually appeared to me to last." Later, however, she is convinced of the brevity of the episodes, since she has to stand "but an instant" before Miss Jessel vanishes in Seizure 5, and, confronting Miss Jessel again in Seizure 6, she can specify, "While these instants lasted."

During some of these "matters" of hers, her hearing as well as her vision is affected in a way that produces in her and in her readers, too, almost the weirdest sensation of all. When Quint rather than the bachelor of Harley Street appears to materialize before her on the tower, her surroundings instantly become a solitude, "all the rest of the scene" seems "stricken with death," an "intense hush" falls, the friendly hour loses "all its voice." Even the rooks stop cawing.

Similarly, watching Flora beside the lake and expecting the child to betray that she shares her governess' impending vision of Miss Jessel, "I held my breath while I waited for what a cry from her . . . would tell me. I waited, but nothing came; then in the first place—and there is something more dire in this, I feel, than in anything I have to relate— I was determined by a sense that within a minute all spontaneous sounds from her had dropped." This narrator *does* make a point of the absence of sound—first the intense hush of Seizure 1 and now the sudden, "dire" silence of the little girl. How long this silence seems to the governess to be preserved she does not relate, though some pages after the episode she reviews (in Chapter VIII) how the child interrupts the spell with renewed activity and sound.

The eeriest hush of all envelops Seizure 4. As the governess stands at the top of the stairs, persuaded that she is facing Quint's ghost, she does not scream, as a less courageous (and more normal?) young woman might have. No, it was

> . . . the dead silence of our long gaze . . . that gave the whole horror, huge as it was, its only note of the unnatural. If I had met a murderer in such a place and at such an hour we still at least would have spoken. Something would have passed, in life, between us; if nothing had passed one of us would have moved. The moment was so prolonged that it would have taken but little more to make me doubt if even *I* were in life. I can't express what followed it save by saying that the silence itself . . . became the element into which I saw the figure disappear.

Rooted to the spot, staring, motionless, soundless, in a state of animation suspended so long that she doubts whether she herself stands among the quick—her exposition, for all its extravagance and art, could almost be said to contain a reasonably accurate report of a trance.

One other theme running through several seizures must be treated. Already quoted is the mention of the cold, faint twilight of earliest dawn, when she undergoes her experience with Quint on the stairs. But in this connection she does not make nearly so much of coldness as she does elsewhere. The "dawn of alarm" which Quint's intrusion on the tower induces apropos of Seizure 1 is "a comparatively human chill, but his second invasion of the premises really sends the temperature down. Entering the formal dining room, "that cold clean temple of mahogany and brass," she fancies she sees him at the window, catches her breath, and turns cold. Convinced that she stands face to face with Miss Jessel in Seizure 6, "I had the extraordinary chill of a feeling that it was I who was the intruder." Soon after her final experience with Miss Jessel, in Chapter XX, she feels "an odorous dampness and roughness, chilling and piercing my trouble." Later, though she has managed to make her way back to the house and has even had tea (which should have warmed her up), "I was conscious of a mortal coldness and felt as if I should never again be warm." On the last page of the novel, during her final seizure, she records an astonishing reaction:

"I was so determined to have all my proof that I flashed into ice to challenge him."

In the governess' career at Bly very abnormal reactions, including rivers of tears, hysteria, and well-nigh complete nervous collapse, frequently succeed the chills, the pale, haunted light of the dusk or the dawn, and the eerie silences. In other words, her postseizural behavior also sometimes falls into a pattern. After seeing a strange man of frightening aspect upon the tower, what would an ordinary, normal young woman do? Scream, rush straight into the house to give the alarm, get help, hurry to the tower with reinforcements, try to arrest the intruder? The governess does none of these. She stands rooted as deeply as she is shaken. She cannot guess at how long she turns the mystery over in her mind or how long, "in a confusion of curiosity and dread," she remains at the site of the collision. But the seizure first attacks her in the twilight, and she re-enters the house when darkness has quite closed in.

"Agitation, in the interval" has driven her to a most unusual course: it has "held me and driven me"; in "circling about the place" she estimates she must have walked three miles. At last she goes inside and meets Mrs. Grose, but tells her nothing. In the pleasant hall with Mrs. Grose's eyes upon her (Mrs. Grose has already greeted her with a "good surprised look"), she achieves "an inward revolution," offers a vague excuse for her lateness, and retreats as soon as possible to her room, pleading the beauty of the night and feet wet from the heavy dew. Still she tells nothing of her experience.

Nor does she until after her second round with Quint, when Mrs. Grose surprises her peering through the window as she believes Quint has peered a short time before. Here again she fails to react like a well-balanced twenty-year-old to a vicious, red-headed rogue at the window.

A sensible girl would probably raise the house with healthy screams for help, flee *from* the dreadful sight, resign her post at the earliest possible moment (once being quite enough and twice being far too often), and quit Bly forthwith. Instead, the governess does extraordinary things. Though "beyond all doubt already far gone," she registers "a sudden vibration of duty and courage," bounds not in the opposite direction but straight out of the room and out of the house, races along the terrace, turns a corner, and comes full in sight—of nothing. It all sounds quite as strenuous as being driven to trudge three miles around the premises by the agitation of Seizure 1. Later comes the collapse. After a disjointed, hysterical conference with Mrs. Grose, the governess is left "prostrate" for an hour, after which she and the housekeeper hold "a little service" of tears, vows, prayers, promises, mutual challenges, and pledges.

Two hours elapse between the time the governess first sees Miss Jessel beside the lake and the time she is able to find her confidante; yet she "can give no intelligible account of how I fought out the interval." Once she finds Mrs. Grose, however, details abound. She throws herself into Mrs. Grose's arms. She can "scarce articulate" and looks "prodigious things." She tries to wring from Mrs. Grose more information about Miss Jessel, but at the end of the inquisition shows "a front of miserable defeat." As her "power to resist" collapses, she bursts into tears, she falls on Mrs. Grose's bosom, her "lamentation" overflows, and she sobs in despair.

The pattern continues after her final experience with Miss Jessel at the lake. When Flora, Mrs. Grose, and what the governess takes to be Miss Jessel's spectre have departed, of "what first happened when I was left alone I had no subsequent memory. I only knew that at the end of, I suppose, a quarter of an hour, an odorous dampness . . . had made me understand that I must have thrown myself, on my face, to the ground and given way to a wildness of grief. I must have lain there long and cried and wailed, for when I raised my head the day was almost done." Here her surrender to hysteria, and to nervous and physical collapse, is complete. The more numerous the seizures become, the more violent their aftermaths.

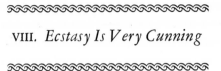

VIII. *Ecstasy Is Very Cunning*

L ISTED in the preceding section are the eight seizures that are most clearly definable. In half of these the governess is persuaded she confronts the ghost of Peter Quint, in the other half the ghost of Miss Jessel. Most but not all of the episodes are marked by certain symptoms, motifs, themes (call them what you will) which repeat themselves— notably the weird silences, the sudden accesses of cold, and the governess' anticipation, her "vivid expectation." Now, what if some of these recur when the governess does *not* contend that Quint and Miss Jessel are appearing to her? Do the symptoms nevertheless signal other attacks, of a somewhat different kind, but attacks all the same? We think they may, and should like to adduce the evidence pointing in this direction.

One of the most inexplicable and uncanny episodes occupies most of Chapter XVII, between Seizures 6 (Miss Jessel in the schoolroom) and 7 (Miss Jessel at the lake a second time). Sleepless, in a state of great tension as usual, the governess listens to the lashing rain and gusts of wind, sits in an effort to write her employer "for a long time before a blank sheet of paper" (compare the possibly hypnogenic effect of prolonged reading and fancy work), then goes into the hall for one of her wonted late nocturnal prowls. When Miles hears her and invites her into his room, a very tense scene ensues. She cross-examines him about his past, an ironical pursuit since he is only ten; she throws herself upon him, embraces him, kisses him; she drops on her knees beside his bed. Her behavior is altogether hysterical. Next, "I knew in a moment . . . I had gone too far. The answer to my appeal was instantaneous but it came in the form of an extraordinary blast and chill, a gust of frozen air and a shake of the room. . . . The boy gave a loud high shriek." Since he is not the shrieking kind anywhere else in the book, but the governess often is, one wonders whether the shriek didn't come from her. Then she becomes aware that it is dark, the curtains are still drawn, and the window tight.

If she sees and reports accurately, the blast and chill have no relation to the batter of the wind and rain to which she has referred earlier, for the window is still closed and the draperies undisturbed. Miles explains the darkness by saying he blew the candle out (one thinks of the dark rooms into which for centuries lunatics were thrust to quiet them), and there seems no reason to doubt his explanation. The implication of the governess' "I knew in a moment I had gone too far" is that Miles's evil, ghostly cohort has chosen blast, chill, frozen air, and shaking room as his supernatural way of interrupting his virtuous adversary's contentions for Miles's soul. But the extraordinary chill and gust of frozen air strike a familiar note and may well herald yet another seizure. Though she does not "see" Quint here, she implies his presence.

On still other occasions, in Chapter XIII, she is overwhelmed with the conviction that both he and Miss Jessel are at hand, communing with the children, but invisible to her. For some time she has feared that "my eyes might be sealed just while theirs were most opened," and she is indeed exempt from direct "vision" for weeks. Repeatedly when she is alone with Miles and Flora, however, she is "ready to swear that, literally, in my presence, but with my direct sense of it closed," the children have visitors who are "known . . . and welcome" to them.

Not to dwell for the moment on the particulars of how Miles and Flora act during these weird sessions, one might do well to concentrate on the governess, keeping a careful eye out for the usual symptoms. And, lo, the appalling silences again descend. Tempted overtly to accuse the children of the supernatural intercourse of which she believes them guilty, she turns crimson, buries her face in her hands, then chatters "more than ever, going on volubly enough till one of our prodigious palpable hushes occurred—I can call them nothing else— the strange dizzy lift or swim (I try for terms!) into a stillness, a pause of all life, that had nothing to do with the more or less noise we at the moment might be engaged in making and that I could hear through any intensified mirth or quickened recitation or louder strum of the piano. Then it was that the others, the outsiders, were there."

Nonapparitionists are tempted mentally to revise her last sentence: "Then it was that I was in the grip of further seizures." The language she employs to describe these episodes creates an effect quite as weird as the silenced rooks and deathly hush attending Quint on the tower or the silence which becomes the element into which he vanishes upon the stairs.

During these times with the children does she also suffer from the chill that characterizes other attacks? Indeed she does—metaphorically perhaps, but the word is there: "such things naturally left on the surface, for the time, a chill that we vociferously denied we felt." The second question to be posed before one passes from "such things" (they cannot be numbered or arranged in chronological order—she simply tells that they are habitual and transpire over a period of a month) to other matters is whether they are connected with what Edmund Parish calls "vivid expectation." Again the answer is yes.

In all fairness, one should mention the difference between the consequences of her expectation in the episodes being considered and in, say, Seizure 1. In the latter she expects to see the master and sees Quint instead. Prior to the scenes described above, her expectation of seeing Quint or Miss Jessel is equally vivid, but she sees nothing—she is only "ready to swear" that they are present whether she sees them or not. Poor girl, her nerves and mind *do* treat her to nasty surprises. The important thing to mark is that the pattern is clearly defined: she palpitates with vivid expectations, then she suffers consequent seizures during which she believes Quint and Miss Jessel either materialize or make their presences felt to her.

A scene between the governess and Mrs. Grose at the end of Chapter XII may have a direct bearing on the fact that the governess expects Quint and Miss Jessel to appear again to her in Chapter XIII but then only "senses" them. As her theories and her explanation of these to the startled Mrs. Grose grow more frenzied, the housekeeper insists that their employer must be summoned to come and take the children away. She is very urgent about this; her insistence amounts, in fact, to a threat: "Their uncle must do the preventing. He must take them away. . . . Make him at any rate come to you. . . . He ought to *be* here— he ought to help." All this threatens the governess' pride—her entire posture at Bly: "She didn't know—no one knew—how proud I had been to serve him and to stick to our terms." She meets Mrs. Grose's threat with one of her own, to leave "on the spot both him and you." After this bristling little conflict she does not *see* Quint or Miss Jessel for a month. It is almost as if she were afraid to do so, afraid to push Mrs. Grose further, daring to give herself only to a more limited experience with her alleged adversaries. She might almost have exclaimed, with Macbeth, "But no more sights!"

Yet the expectations which follow in Chapter XIII and which she is evidently unable to suppress are as vivid as any to be found in the novel:

The fact that the days passed for me without another encounter ought . . . to have done something toward soothing my nerves. Since the light brush . . . of the presence of a woman at the foot of the stair [Seizure 5], I had seen nothing, whether in or out of the house, that one had better not have seen. There was many a corner round which I expected to come upon Quint, and many a situation that, in a merely sinister way, would have favoured the appearance of Miss Jessel. . . . There were exactly states of the air, conditions of sound and of stillness [again], unspeakable impressions of the *kind* of ministering moment, that brought back to me, long enough to catch it, the feeling of the medium in which, that June evening out of doors, I had had my first sight of Quint [Seizure 1], and in which too, at those other instants, I had, after seeing him through the window [Seizure 2], looked for him in vain in the circle of shrubbery. I recognized the signs, the portents—I recognized the moment, the spot. But they remained unaccompanied and empty, and I continued unmolested; if unmolested one could call a young woman whose sensibility had, in the most extraordinary fashion, not declined but deepened. . . . What I had . . . had an ugly glimpse of was that my eyes might be sealed just while theirs were most opened. Well, my eyes *were* sealed, it appeared, at present—a consummation for which it seemed blasphemous not to thank God. There was, alas, a difficulty about that: I would have thanked him with all my soul had I not had in a proportionate measure this conviction of the secret of my pupils.

Their secret, she thinks, is that they now entertain Quint and Miss Jessel in the very presence of their governess. Though her eyes may be sealed, other vaguely defined senses are freely operative. She is as tortured by only sensing the fiends' visitations as she is by seeing them. As for the pain the various degrees and kinds of seizures inflict upon her, there is little to choose between them.

The expectations which the governess has been allowed to reveal at some length above are all of a piece with those which preface other seizures. Consider for example the preamble to Seizure 3 in Chapter VI: "I had an absolute certainty that I should see again what I had already seen [i.e., Quint, in Seizures 1 and 2] . . . that by offering myself bravely as the sole subject of such experience, by accepting, by inviting, by surmounting it all, I should . . . guard the tranquillity of the rest of the household." The phrase "by inviting" is arresting and raises the question whether these recurrent preludes to her seizures should not be termed "invitations" rather than "expectations."

The governess continues, a little later in the chapter when she is actually at the site of Seizure 3 with Flora beside the lake: "Suddenly . . . I became aware that on the other side . . . we had an interested spectator. The way this knowledge gathered in me was the strangest thing in the world." She begins "to take in with certitude and yet without direct vision the presence, a good way off, of a third person." This *is* strange. She has no direct vision, the apparition is at a distance, yet she is certain: there is "no ambiguity in anything; none whatever at least in the conviction I from one moment to another found myself forming as to what I should see straight before me and across the lake as a consequence of raising my eyes." She instantly, passionately, questions the "right of presence" of this figure—which she has not seen yet, please remember. She keeps her eyes on her stitching until she has sufficiently steadied herself to decide what to do. She considers the chances that the figure may turn out to be one of the men about the place, a messenger, postman, or tradesman's boy. But she rejects these possibilities, "still even without looking." They have "little effect on my practical certitude."

In other words, she will *not* be deflected from conjuring up a dreadful sight. She has expected to see one, she has invited it to appear, and see it she will. She is in for another nasty shock, for when she at last raises her eyes she descries, not the usual image, but the female figure whom she identifies as Miss Jessel.

IX. *Seeing and Not Seeing*

THE GOVERNESS' final encounter with Miss Jessel occupies Chapters XIX and XX. The central action of this experience recalls the plain, garden variety of seizure in which the governess expects to see one of her pair of evil demons and is not disappointed. To summarize briefly, while Miles is diverting the governess by playing the piano, Flora disappears. After a vain search of the house in which she is joined by Mrs. Grose, the governess announces that Flora is with Miss Jessel at a distance. "I had made up my mind." She drags the house-keeper off to verify her announcement. As always, her expectations come true—for her, at least—when she believes she catches sight of the ghostly image standing upon the opposite bank of the lake "exactly as she had stood the other time." Her problem is that the objectivity of the apparition remains unvalidated by Mrs. Grose and Flora (and consequently incredible to the nonapparitionist). Try as she may, Mrs. Grose can see nothing, and Flora heatedly denies that she sees anything or ever has. For the first (and last) time the governess has suffered an attack in the presence of another adult. She feels "my own situation horribly crumble."

The physical actions leading to this debacle are worth tracing because for nonapparitionists they contain the clue to still another kind of seizure, one that has hitherto escaped notice. Until this episode the governess habitually senses or sees what is not there; here, we believe, she fails to see what *is* there. But to begin at the beginning, Mrs. Grose leaves the house with reluctance to accompany the governess on her searching expedition. Without wraps they sally forth into the damp, gray afternoon and make straight for the lake. The progress of their search is not steady, however, because James interrupts it to expend many words on the lake,

as it was called at Bly, and I dare say rightly called, though it may have been a sheet of water less remarkable than my untraveled eyes supposed it. My acquaintance with sheets of water was small, and the pool of Bly, at all events on the few occasions of my consenting, under the protection of my pupils, to affront its surface in the old flat-bottomed boat moored there for our use, had impressed me both with its extent and its agitation. The usual place of embarkation was half a mile from the house. . . . there was no trace of Flora on that nearer side of the bank . . . and none on the opposite edge, where, save for a margin of some twenty yards, a thick copse came down to the pond. This expanse, oblong in shape, was so narrow compared to its length that, with its ends out of view, it might have been taken for a scant river.

Now, James is not much given to extensive descriptions of nature and the general topography of the estate at Bly. To find him interrupting such a breathless scene with all this talk of the lake is therefore a little startling, especially when one remembers his insistence, in his famous preface, that he fought so hard for "every grudged inch of space" in writing *The Turn of the Screw* that it contains not a superfluous inch. If we take him at his word, then the rather prolonged passage about the lake is not irrelevant or aimless: James wrote it with a purpose, and this we believe to be revealed in what follows.

As the two women stand upon the bank with no Flora in sight, the governess says, "She has taken the boat," whereupon Mrs. Grose stares "at the vacant mooring-place." How are they to continue their urgent search on the other side of the lake without the old flat-bottomed boat which, with a few strokes of the oars, could carry them across the expanse James has very carefully defined as "so narrow . . . that . . . it might have been taken for a scant river"? There is but one alternative, the governess decides, and she starts "to walk further," down the length of the lake which James has also painstakingly described as considerable when compared with its width. This action elicits from Mrs. Grose the incredulous question, "By going all the way round?" Clearly she is unwilling to join the governess in the hike; it is only "the chain of my logic," so the governess thinks, that drags Mrs. Grose "at my heels even now."

Why is Mrs. Grose hesitant to take the long way round? Granted, she is no longer young or built for hiking; still she is as eager as the governess to recover Flora, if not more so. The explanation of her reluctance is a simple one: there is no need to walk at all. Flora has of course *not* taken the boat. When the governess states that she has, Mrs. Grose stares "at the vacant mooring-place" because it is *not* vacant. Before the very eyes of her confidante the governess, by failing to see what is there, betrays her derangement. There is only one more shocking way to betray it, and James employs that way before the episode closes. Before the very eyes of Mrs. Grose *and* Flora, the governess sees what is *not* there—what she takes to be Miss Jessel's spectre.

The passage concerning the boat and the hike deserves further quotation, for only this will convey the full flavor of the various ironies involved, of the shocks Mrs. Grose experiences, and of the subtlety and craft of James's art:

We looked at the empty stretch, and then I felt the suggestion in my friend's eyes. I knew what she meant and I replied with a negative headshake.

"No, no; wait! She has taken the boat."

My companion stared at the vacant mooring-place and then again across the lake. "Then where is it?"

"Our not seeing it is the strongest of proofs. She has used it to go over and then has managed to hide it."

"All alone—that child?"

"She's not alone, and at such times she's not a child: she's an old, old woman." I scanned all the visible shore while Mrs. Grose took again, into the queer element I offered her, one of her plunges of submission; then I pointed out that the boat might perfectly be in a small refuge formed by one of the recesses of the pool, an indentation masked, for the hither side, by a projection of the bank and by a clump of trees growing close to the water.

"But if the boat's there, where on earth's *she?*" my colleague anxiously asked.

"That's exactly what we must learn." And I started to walk further.

"By going all the way round?"

"Certainly, far as it is. It will take us but ten minutes, yet it's far enough to have made the child prefer not to walk. She went straight over."

"Laws!" cried my friend again: the chain of my logic was ever too strong for her. It dragged her at my heels even now, and when we had got half-way round—a devious tiresome process, on ground much broken and by a path choked with overgrowth—I paused to give her breath. I sustained her with a grateful arm, assuring her that she might hugely help me; and this started us afresh, so that in the course of but few minutes more we reached a point from which we found the boat to be where I had supposed it. It had been intentionally left as much as possible out of sight and was tied to one of the stakes of a fence that came, just there, down to the brink and that had been an assistance to disembarking. I recognised, as I looked at the pair of short thick oars, quite safely drawn up, the prodigious character of the feat for a little girl.

Notice the ironies which emerge in the light of the reading we advocate. What must have gone through the mind of Mrs. Grose, for whom the mooring-place is *not* vacant, when the governess says of the boat, "Our not seeing it is the strongest of proofs," especially at the words "our," "strongest," and "proofs"? There is still more irony in the governess' construing her companion's scandalized "Laws!" as Mrs. Grose's surrender to "the chain of my logic." Logic indeed! With her dumbfounded questions and shocked exclamation Mrs. Grose is in effect refusing to deny the evidence of her own eyes, to accept the governess' mad theorizing, and to join cheerfully in an unnecessary trek. In effect she is asking, "Do you mean that you insist on our reaching the other side by going all the way round, taking that long, difficult, ten-minute walking tour when we could be across in two minutes by getting into the boat and rowing a few strokes with the oars?" When the governess does indeed insist with "Certainly, far as it is," it is no wonder Mrs. Grose exclaims "Laws!" Like the Flora of the governess' wild hypothesis, Mrs. Grose prefers not to walk but to go straight over.

Observe also how James, again unwontedly pausing over the details of nature, underlines the difficulty of the safari in the rest of the paragraph. The governess' "logic" drags Mrs. Grose at her heels through the "devious tiresome process, on ground much broken and by a path choked with overgrowth." So arduous is the journey that the governess pauses half way around to let the elder woman catch her breath, which appears to be sufficiently spent to require the governess to support her "with a grateful arm." James thus makes the insanity of the trek as clear to a wary reader as he does to Mrs. Grose.

The alternative interpretation of these events is of course the governess', which sounds stark, staring mad in résumé: Miles and Flora devise, with devilish ingenuity, to frustrate their governess' eternal vigilance by Miles's piano playing so that Flora may slip away for her rendezvous with the ghost of Miss Jessel. The ghost and the child—though "at such times she's not a child: she's an old, old woman"—row the old flat-bottomed boat (each plying an oar?) across the lake, secrete it in a cove conveniently masked by trees and a projection of the bank, and thus secure for themselves a chance to carry on, clandestinely, afar, without fear of immediate interruption, their abominable communion. Oh, Laws, Laws, Laws!

The rest of the episode concerning the boat falls into the old familiar pattern. Though the governess at first fails to see the boat in its mooring place, she confidently expects she *will* see it shortly in the certain small cove on the far side of the lake. Sure enough, the boat turns out "to be where I had supposed it." Frenzied though she is, even the governess, as she "looks at" the short, thick oars, recognizes "the prodigious character of the feat for a little girl." For the sake of completeness, one might mention finally that as they depart from the cove and catch sight of Flora, they approach her "in a silence by this time flagrantly ominous." After previous citations of silence, how can one be sure that in this context it represents only a kind of tripartite tension, suspense, or sulkiness?

x. *Mystification Kneaded Thick*

IN HIS preface of 1908 James discusses one of his intentions regarding *The Turn of the Screw*. "The study is of a conceived 'tone' . . . the tone of tragic, yet of exquisite mystification." His chief endeavor was "to knead the subject of my young friend's, the suppositious narrator's, mystification thick, and yet strain the expression of it so clear and fine that beauty would result." The "so many intense anomalies and obscurities" which James imposes upon her are not only numerous but often complex, though some may be simply put. For example, why may Miles not return to his school; what precisely were Quint and Miss Jessel like; what exactly was their relationship to each other and to the children?

Another problem with which she must perpetually grapple—and one which has received almost no attention—is the question of her own sanity. About this matter apparitionists have far fewer doubts than the governess herself. For once, these doubts do not constitute a burden she must bear alone. Mrs. Grose obviously shares them from time to time. First, let us review the abnormality of the governess' reactions to Seizures 1 and 2. Where a girl who felt she could believe her own eyes

would have rushed for help and poured out her story at the earliest opportunity, the governess circles Bly in her agitation, and when she finally enters the house after dark and meets Mrs. Grose she tells the
housekeeper—nothing whatsoever.

She rationalizes her failure to do so as "the instinct of sparing my
companion." One imagines that she may have spared her knowledge of
Seizure 2 as well had not Mrs. Grose surprised her staring in the window. Why not tell all to the only responsible adult available for confidences? Because, the nonapparitionist argues, she does *not* trust her own
eyes; she suspects she has suffered an hallucination and is afraid to confess it to Mrs. Grose. If so, her euphemism—her instinct to "spare" her
companion—takes on ironic overtones. That she herself considers the
possibility of aberration is shown by a sentence which crops up in the
aftermath of Seizure 1: after hours of agitated mental threshing about,
unable to arrive at any "account whatever of the visitor with whom I
had been so inexplicably and yet . . . so intimately concerned," she
then records, "There was but one sane inference," namely, that "some
unscrupulous traveler . . . had made his way in unobserved." It is interesting that she should use the word "sane" in this context. The implication is that its antonym has also crossed her mind.

She is faced with a distressing choice, especially when the seizures
begin to multiply—either I am seeing ghosts or having hallucinations.
She chooses the former explanation, naturally, and tries her best to
cleave to it. But simply trying is not enough. She desperately longs for
the confirmation of another witness, the corroboration of a second pair
of eyes. That is why her reaction to Seizure 7, as she stands beside the
lake with Mrs. Grose and Flora, strikes some readers as distinctly odd,
while it makes complete sense to others who have apprehended and ap-
preciated how starved she is for corroboration. As the ghost of Miss
Jessel materializes to her eyes, she writes, "I remember, strangely, as the
first feeling now produced in me, my thrill of joy at having brought on
a proof. She was there, so I was justified; she was there, so I was neither
cruel nor mad."

But Mrs. Grose fails her. The housekeeper sees nothing and says so vehemently. Proof and justification are withheld, and the ravening governess, quailing under "this hard blow" of the proof that her eyes were hopelessly sealed, feels her "situation horribly crumble." While the seizure is in progress, despite her "sense of ruin," she comforts herself with "a sense, touching to me even then, that she would have backed me up if she had been able." There is to be no further, just as there has been no previous, opportunity to gain the good woman's backing, for Seizure 7 is the sole occasion when the governess believes she, Mrs. Grose, and one of the ghosts are present simultaneously.

From first to last, the governess is denied the consolation Hamlet enjoys of being able to prove that others—Horatio, Marcellus, and Bernardo—also see the Danish ghost, whose objectivity is thus firmly established. The ghost of King Hamlet also speaks, and what it has to say is relevant and demonstrably true. The apparitions that the governess "brings on" (to echo her own idiom) are, on the contrary, mute, though she longs so for the evidence of her ears as well as of her eyes that she sometimes puts into words what the postures, gestures, attitudes, and glares of Quint and Miss Jessel seem to her to express.

To illustrate the point that the governess writhes under this particular mystification literally until the end of the story, here is a passage from the last chapter. As she is in the act of frightening Miles to death, "the appalling alarm of his being perhaps innocent" assails her, and she finds the thought "confounding and bottomless, for if he *were* innocent, what then on earth was I?" In this way James insures that she is never liberated from the mystifications which oppress her. It is hard to imagine how he could have devised a more refined torture for a young woman of the governess' temperament.

Her quest for proof and her recurrent self-doubts run through her narrative as themes with copious, subtle variations run through a symphony. In the middle of Seizure 7, as we have seen, she is jubilant at having at last produced a "proof." This is the culmination of who knows how many months of sick longing for such a chance. As early as Chapter XIII, in a lucid moment, she gives her own uncertainty away in the absence of evidence (the italics are ours): "I had then expressed [to Mrs. Grose] what was vividly in my mind: the truth that, *whether the children really saw or not—since, that is, it was not yet definitely proved*—I greatly preferred ... the fulness of my own exposure." One further example of this theme, from Chapter XVIII: "I constantly both attacked and renounced the enigma of what such a little gentleman could have done that deserved a penalty. Say that ... the imagination of all evil *had* been opened up to him: all the justice within me ached for the proof that it could ever have flowered into an act."

Like "proof," the word "mad," or some variation of it, flows often from her pen, as do synonyms or closely related terms. Witness the following illustrations of how often the question of her own sanity crosses her mind.

"I began to watch them in a stifled suspense, a disguised tension that might well, had it continued too long, have turned to something like madness."

After thrusting on Mrs. Grose her grim theory that the children and ghosts perpetually meet, the governess adds, " 'I go on, I know, as if I were crazy; and it's a wonder I'm not. What I've seen would have made *you* so'."

When Mrs. Grose urges writing the bachelor uncle to come fetch the children away,

"[The governess.] 'By writing to him that his house is poisoned and his little nephew and niece mad?'
"[Mrs. Grose.] 'But if they *are*, Miss?'
"[The governess.] 'And if I am myself, you mean?' "

During Seizure 7: "She was there, so I was neither cruel nor mad!"

"There was but one sane inference."

Mrs. Grose "accepted without directly inpugning my sanity the truth as I gave it to her."

Mrs. Grose "addressed her greatest solicitude to the sad case presented by their deputy-guardian."

The governess tells Mrs. Grose that the children's more than earthly beauty is "a game ... a policy and a fraud ... mad as that seems."

The passage of time tends to erase from the governess' mind certain "grievous fancies."

"The schoolroom piano broke into all gruesome fancies."

These comments involving her sanity are widely scattered throughout the novel, from Chapter VI to Chapter XX, from page 467 to page 527. It is worth mentioning that a noticeably large proportion of these suggestive remarks are concentrated in Chapter VI, over half of which is devoid of dialogue, and in Chapter IX, which has no dialogue at all. They are two largely expository sections and afford a wider scope for morbid introspection than the ordinary chapter.

In his preface James asserts that since he was fighting for economy in his tale he had to forego treating the governess in any relationship other than those with which he deals. If he had expanded his treatment, one of the additional relationships would have been that of herself to her own nature. One must agree, certainly, that in general she is not a conspicuous success at following the maxim "Know thyself." Yet she is not altogether ignorant of what makes her tick. Some of the phrases that insinuate themselves casually into her narrative and that are in effect further variations of those just noticed strike the nonapparitionist even as remarkable flashes of self-knowledge. The following are examples:

It was a pity I should have had to quaver out again the reasons for my not having, in my delusion, so much as questioned that the little girl saw our visitant.

It was not, I am as sure today as I was sure then, my mere infernal imagination.

How can I retrace today the strange steps of my obsession?

What, under my endless obsession, I had been impelled to listen for was some betrayal of his not being at rest.

The language here is thought-provoking. Stumbling upon such expressions as "my delusion," "my mere infernal imagination," and "my endless obsession" in the middle of the governess' usual rhapsodies and wild rationalizations, the nonapparitionist suspects that she is at last beginning to call things by their right names.

XI. *Endless Mystifications and Inductions*

UNCERTAINTY concerning her sanity is not the only mystification to cause the governess pain. Somewhere she says that she has more pains than one, which is almost tantamount, from a girl of her curiosity, to saying that she faces more mystifications than one. In addition to "mystification," James uses the words "intense anomalies and obscurities," and he prefers "anxieties" to "pain," though the witness to her relentless search for solutions acceptable to her may think "anxieties" too mild a term.

In his preface James writes, "We have surely as much of her own nature as we can swallow in watching it reflect her anxieties and inductions." He considers already sufficiently engaging "the general proposition of our young woman's keeping crystalline her record of so many intense anomalies and obscurities—*by which I don't of course mean her explanation of them, a different matter"* (italics ours).

A study of her narrative reveals the full significance of James's remarks. Confronted with assorted anxieties, intense anomalies, and obscurities, the governess records them with extraordinary clarity, it is true. But while in the throes of mystification, she makes inductions and offers explanations that are *not* crystalline. They are suspect. The reader is not obliged to accept them. He may even reject them outright—surely James invites him to in the italicized clause—though after doing so he should in all fairness propose alternatives, better, more plausible ones. That any reader can solve all the obscurities in the novel is too much to hope. There is no evidence that James intended to make all of them susceptible of solution and so exempt the reader from the mystification. Since thought is free, however, let us examine the first of the governess' major inductions and possible alternatives to it.

The first serious mystification overtakes her at the beginning of Chapter II when she receives from her employer a note enclosing another, from the headmaster of Miles's school. Since it arrives before she has begun to be plagued by seizures, these cannot be accused of coloring or unbalancing her judgment as she labors with the mystery in a conference with Mrs. Grose:

The Governess. What does it mean? The child's dismissed his school.
Mrs. Grose. But aren't they all—?
The Governess. Sent home—yes. But only for the holidays. Miles may never go back at all.
Mrs. Grose. They won't take him?
The Governess. They absolutely decline.
Mrs. Grose (her eyes filling with tears). What has he done? (Putting her hands behind her as the governess tries to hand her the letter.) Such things are not for me, Miss.
The Governess (opens letter to read it to Mrs. Grose, falters, folds it again, puts it back in her pocket.) Is he really bad?
Mrs. Grose. Do the gentlemen say so?
The Governess. They go into no particulars. They simply express their regret that it should be impossible to keep him.

Based solely on the evidence afforded here, a likely reproduction of the headmaster's letter to Miles's uncle would read as follows:

Dear ———:
We regret that we cannot keep your nephew Miles as a student at ———.

Truly yours,
———(Headmaster)

Since the headmaster goes into "no particulars" we can never know exactly why he wrote the letter; we can only explore a few of the possibilities. There is a clue in the prologue, where Douglas passes along the information that the governess' employer offers her during their first interview. In addition to superintending Flora, the new governess "would also have, in holidays, to look after the small boy, who had been for a term at school—young as he was to be sent [he is 'scarce ten years old,' we learn later], but what else could be done?—and who, as the holidays were about to begin, would be back from one day to the other. There had been for the two children at first a young lady whom they had had the misfortune to lose. She had done for them quite beautifully . . . till her death, the great awkwardness of which had, precisely, left no alternative but the school for little Miles."

If a copy of the uncle's letter making arrangements with the headmaster were extant, it might be illuminating. The data in the prologue allow an enlightened guess that the uncle outlined the predicament Miss Jessel's death had left him in, then appealed to the headmaster to admit his ward despite his extreme youth until other arrangements could be made for the lad's schooling. The headmaster, whom the uncle describes in his note to the governess as "an awful bore," may have consented, at length, to accept the child for a single term after dilating on the inadvisability of sending boys so young away to boarding school and on the numbers of applicants turned away annually. His letter of regret at not being able to keep the boy, now that the uncle has made other arrangements, *could* mean that he regrets the loss of so promising and brilliant a student as Miles (if the governess' extravagant praise of his brilliance is to be taken seriously). All this is mere speculation, of course. But it is not less plausible than the line the governess takes, and certainly it is more charitable.

It would be imprudent to overlook or minimize the stress laid in the prologue upon the tenderness of Miles's years—"young as he was to be sent." In a review of *Thomas Arnold* (1960), T. W. Bamford's book on possibly the greatest of all headmasters, Raymond Mortimer writes, in *The Sunday Times of London*,

Arnold, perhaps wisely, thought that Rugby was no place for boys under twelve, whom it was obliged to accept under the Founder's will. He effectively stopped parents sending such boys by placing them under teachers whom he knew to be incompetent. This was pronounced illegal by the Master of the Rolls, who obtained from the Trustees of the school an assurance of their intention to comply with this judgment. But Arnold was having none of this. What startles me is not so much his continuing to defy the law as the dodge by which he sought to evade it. Having taken boys into his school, he deliberately refused them education. Have we any "great" headmasters today? I rather hope not.

The way the governess' mind is working upon the mystery of the headmaster's letter is evident from her choice of words as she confers with Mrs. Grose. "The child's dismissed his school. . . . Miles may never go back at all. . . . They absolutely decline [to take him back]. . . . Is he really *bad?*" She has either forgotten the uncle's significant remarks about Miles's extreme youth and there being no alternative but to send him off to school, or she prefers to ignore the possibilities implicit in these remarks. Dealing in possibilities, in scholarly subjunctives and perhapses is not her way. "They go into no particulars. They simply express their regret that it should be impossible to keep him. That can have only one meaning." One gasps at the "induction" in the last sentence, and gasps again when she proclaims what the meaning is —"That he's an injury to the others."

After so "concluding" on page 448, she reverses her opinion on page 459 and decides the boy was expelled because "he was only too fine and fair for the little horrid unclean school-world." This breathtaking aboutface might be more gratifying if her condemnation of Miles were not replaced by her blanket condemnation of the entire world of secondary education. Little horrid unclean Eton, Harrow, and Rugby. How the headmaster of Miles's school, not to mention Dr. Arnold, would have rubbed his eyes!

But the governess does not permit the burden of guilt—if there is any—to rest on the stately shoulders of the public school Miles has left. She continues to grapple with the mystery and to shift the reprehension about. Vacillating is as typical of her as are thinking the worst and jumping to conclusions. Because the mystery begotten by the head-master's letter is at first uncomplicated by seizures, it is a good one to pursue through the novel. "We have surely as much of her own nature as we can swallow in watching it reflect her anxieties and inductions," James writes. Very well, then; her anxieties and inductions about Miles's schooling, past and present, should be worth tracing.

Mrs. Grose has known the boy all his life and at least two genera-tions of his family before him (she has formerly been maid to his grandmother). Her reaction therefore is more creditable than the first induction of the governess, who has never clapped eyes on him. *The Governess*: "That can have only one meaning. . . . That he's an injury to the others." *Mrs. Grose* (suddenly flaring up): "Master Miles! *him* an injury? . . . It's too dreadful . . . to say such cruel things! Why, he's scarce ten years old." So the induction is "dreadful" and "cruel" in the opinion of one better qualified to judge the child than his accuser. In the face of Mrs. Grose's vehemence the governess' baseless induction crum-bles. She says, "Yes, yes; it would be incredible," and lets the matter drop—until further along on the same page. Here, her morbid curi-osity overpowering her again, she begins a fresh inquisition of Mrs. Grose, who has, not surprisingly, been trying to avoid her and who has "clearly, by this time, and very honestly, adopted an attitude," the sort of attitude any sane person adopts toward the perpetration of irrational, cruel charges.

The Governess. I take what you said to me at noon as a declaration that *you've* never known him to be bad.
Mrs. Grose (throwing back her head). Oh never known him— I don't pre-tend *that*!
The Governess ("upset again"). Then you *have* known him—?
Mrs. Grose. Yes indeed, Miss, thank God!
The Governess. You mean that a boy who never is—?
Mrs. Grose. Is no boy for me!
The Governess. You like them with the spirit to be naughty? So do I! But not to the degree to contaminate—
Mrs. Grose. To contaminate?

The Governess. To corrupt.
Mrs. Grose. (with an odd laugh). Are you afraid he'll corrupt *you*?

Mrs. Grose clearly gets the better of this interview. Her final sally reduces the governess to "a laugh, a little silly doubtless, to match her own," and the governess gives way "for the time to the apprehension of ridicule."

Though Mrs. Grose's ridicule only temporarily deflects the inquisitor, Miles's actual appearance convinces her of his innocence. Happily, if the old proverb "You can't tell a book by its binding" was quoted at the parsonage, she does not recall it at Bly. Finding Miles incredibly beautiful, she is "merely bewildered" and "outraged—by the sense of the horrible letter locked up in one of the drawers of my room." As soon as she can manage a private word with (the still elusive?) Mrs. Grose, she declares that "it" is "grotesque." *Mrs. Grose*: "You mean the cruel charge—?" *The Governess*: "It doesn't live an instant. My dear woman, *look* at him!" Mrs. Grose now presses her: "What will you say then?" The governess assures her that she will say nothing of the grotesque induction to the headmaster, the uncle, or Miles. Mrs. Grose, who has not yet learned the meaning of the word vacillation, accepts the governess' assurance, and promises to stand by her.

Here, one might think, a reasonable woman would let the matter drop. Surely nothing in Miles's conduct would serve to resurrect the governess' appalling theory. Soon she is able to declare that after being with the children for a time she can "face that mystery without a pang" —an ironic phrase in the light of the pangs she suffers before our eyes from pages 451 through 549 (the next to the last in the novel) in struggling with this mystery alone. Miles himself, she decides, has "cleared it up" and made "the whole charge absurd." He never mentions school, a comrade, or a master, but the governess is "quite too much disgusted to allude to them." For they are, please remember, little, horrid and unclean, including "even stupid sordid headmasters" (*pace* Dr. Arnold). And so her "conclusion bloomed there with the real rose-flush of his innocence," she writes, with a floridity unusual even for her. Adulation has, temporarily, replaced condemnation. Yet it does not serve to put an end to her brooding. On the same page she notes that "deep obscurity" continues "to cover the region of the boy's conduct at school."

The "conclusion" which has just rosily bloomed wilts on pages 480 through 483, where she again subjects Mrs. Grose to an austere inquiry lasting almost three pages. The gist of this interrogation is "What was it you had in mind when . . . you said . . . that you didn't pretend . . . he had not literally *ever* been 'bad'? . . . What was your exception . . . ?" She is like a relentless bloodhound who returns, baying, to the scent. It is a remarkably faint one since Miles "has *not* truly 'ever,' in these weeks that I myself have lived with him and so closely watched him; he has been an imperturbable little prodigy of delightful loveable goodness." The scene contains a hint that Mrs. Grose is again an unwilling witness; it is unconscionably late when the governess gets her answer "before the grey dawn" admonishes them to separate.

Mrs. Grose's answer, when it comes, is confused, partly because the governess interrupts, carries on the questioning in language often incomprehensible to Mrs. Grose, and as usual jumps to conclusions. Saving the details of Mrs. Grose's testimony for future discussion, let us note only that she has "unreservedly . . . forgiven him," probably because there is little to forgive, that in her opinion he is "Ah nothing that's not nice *now*," and that her last word on the subject is, "Surely you don't accuse *him*—," a sentence she never has a chance to finish, the governess finishing it for her. Though lacking evidence, the governess concludes that Miles has "lied and been impudent" to Mrs. Grose. The rose of his innocence now lies scentless and dead.

As Miles continues to radiate obvious sweetness, goodness, and intellectual brilliance, the governess gains an "unnatural composure on the subject of another school" for him. Yet she also continues to regard it as a "mystification without end" for "such a boy to have been 'kicked out' by a school-master." Observe that she persists in entertaining no other theory than that he was expelled for cause. Despite her persistence, however, she is able, in the children's company, to "follow no scent very far." Poor baffled bloodhound. In time even their company fails to soothe her, so that, evidence or no evidence, she manages to seize on a comment of Miles's, "Think, you know, what I *might* do," and say to Mrs. Grose, "He knows down to the ground what he 'might' do. That's what he gave them a taste of at school."

It should be recalled that at their last interview on the subject the governess has promised Mrs. Grose to say nothing to the headmaster, uncle, or boy, but to drop the "cruel," "dreadful," "grotesque," and "incredible" charge. When the governess here revives it, Mrs. Grose has good reason to cry, "Lord, you do change!" It is only fair to add that by this time the governess has suffered at least five seizures which of course do little to augment her powers of reasoning. She has succeeded in connecting the mystery of the "apparitions" with that of Miles's "expulsion" (her word): wicked Quint; wicked, expelled Miles; wicked Flora (guilty by association); wicked Miss Jessel—"The four, depend upon it, perpetually meet."

The headmaster expresses regret "that it should be impossible to keep" Miles: his letter has goaded her a long way down her irrational, evil-seeking path. Her direct dealings with Miles about his education deserve separate treatment. Here it is enough to record a few scattered but typical passages showing how, until almost the moment Miles dies in her arms, she adheres to her conviction that he has been expelled from school for wickedness. Eventually Miles's attitude—and she pronounces him "immensely in the right"—grows to be, "Either you clear up with my guardian the mystery of this interruption of my studies, or you cease to expect me to lead with you a life that's so unnatural for a boy." Yet she still fears "having to deal with the intolerable question of the grounds of his dismissal from school," though a conference with the uncle is "a solution that, strictly speaking, I ought now" to precipitate. Why should she fear to confer unless she has more than an inkling of the speciousness of her own explanation of Miles's "dismissal"?

Even so, she refuses to relinquish the theory. She decides to have things out with her employer:

The Governess. Yes, yes; his uncle shall have it here from me on the spot (and before the boy himself if necessary) that if I'm to be reproached with having done nothing again about more school—

Mrs. Grose. Yes, Miss—

The Governess. Well, there's that awful reason.

Mrs. Grose. But—a—which?

The Governess. Why the letter from his old place.

Mrs. Grose. You'll show it to the master?

The Governess. I ought to have done so on the instant.

Mrs. Grose. Oh no!

The Governess. I'll put it before him that I can't undertake to work the question on behalf of a child who has been expelled—

Mrs. Grose. For we've never in the least known what!

The Governess. For wickedness. For what else—when he's so clever and beautiful and perfect? Is he stupid? Is he untidy? Is he infirm? Is he ill-natured? He's exquisite—so it can be only *that*.

Miraculous Miles—to be simultaneously exquisite, perfect, and wicked! Since his perfection is consistently in evidence, his wickedness never, the governess has "perpetually . . . to check the irrelevant gaze and discouraged sigh" in which she constantly attacks "the enigma of what such a little gentleman could have done that deserved a penalty"; and "all the justice within" her aches for the "proof that it [the evil within him] could ever have flowered into an act." After this admission that she lacks proof and still faces an enigma, the reader feels hopeful of a return to sanity. Here, at least, is a passage that does not bristle with the cocksureness that usually attends her inductions.

Soon she returns to her old ways. Some twenty-two pages after she has promised to write the uncle, we discover that her letter to him has never been posted. It disappears from the hall table and thus breeds a new mystery. Who took it? The governess edges toward one of her typical inductions in the following:

Mrs. Grose. Your letter never went.

The Governess. What then became of it?

Mrs. Grose. Goodness knows! Master Miles—

The Governess. Do you mean *he* took it? . . . [If so] he probably will have read it and destroyed it. . . .

Mrs. Grose. I make out now what he must have done at school. (She gives "an almost droll disillusioned nod.") He stole!
The Governess. Well—perhaps.
Mrs. Grose. He stole *letters*!

Observe that the notion that Miles is a thief occurs first to the governess. Mrs. Grose's droll nod and preposterous suggestion indicate her understanding of the governess' usual mental leaps. She is treating the governess as one treats a lunatic who has already shown herself beyond recall. She says, in effect, "At last you've got at the truth of it. He's a wretched, wicked little letter-stealer. *That*'s why they expelled him." The governess, after trying "to be more judicial" with her "Well—perhaps," adopts Mrs. Grose's "solution," which she herself has initiated: "I hope then that it was to more purpose [at school] than in this case! The note . . . will have given him so scant an advantage . . . that he's already much ashamed . . . and that what he had on his mind last evening was precisely the need of confession."

It is important to bear in mind that the question for her has long since ceased to be "Why did the headmaster regret that it should be impossible to keep him?" She asks herself only, "For what particular wickedness was Miles expelled?" Almost her final bout with the insoluble occurs at dinner with him, just before he dies. "Whatever he had been expelled from school for, it wasn't for ugly feeding."

She learns the "truth" at last, from Miles's own lips, in the last chapter. Here Miles struggles so agonizingly to appease her with details of his wickedness at school that one suspects there are no details and no wickedness to describe. This possibility obviously crosses the governess' mind also. As she strives to wring blood from the little turnip, "for pure tenderness" she shakes him "as if to ask him why, if it was all for nothing, he had condemned me to months of torment." Mark Van Doren is right in asserting that the governess "is forced by the irony of her character and fate to torture this little boy into confessions which he doesn't want to make, which he doesn't even know how to make because he has nothing to confess."

The governess' approach to the mystery concerning Miles's school is

typical of her way of thinking for two reasons. First, she jumps to conclusions despite a paucity or total absence of evidence. From time to
time she calls this method "intuitive," "logical," and "inspired," and
there is irony in James's choice of all three adjectives. Second, her conclusion is predicated upon the conviction that the world is a sinful,
wicked place full of sinful, wicked people. She does not, in a word, allow one to forget she is the daughter of a country parson.

The same suspicious, puritanical cast of mind is evident in minor as
well as major "inductions." Concerning the bachelor, whom she sees
only twice: "She figured him as rich, but as fearfully extravagant" and
possibly not as particular as he might be in his choice of servants and
female companions. Concerning the hearty welcome Mrs. Grose ac-
cords her when they first meet: instead of rejoicing at "her being so
inordinately glad to see me," the governess perceives that she is "so
glad . . . as to be positively on her guard against showing it too much"
and wonders "why she should wish not to show it, and that, with reflexion, with suspicion, might of course have made me uneasy." The
whole process makes the reader uneasy too: extravagant, insufficiently
fastidious employer and disingenuous Mrs. Grose—both condemned
without a fair trial.

While professing to be pleased and impressed with Miles's intellectual aptitude, the governess "might have got" the impression, she says,
that his brilliance is due to "some influence operating in his small intellectual life as a tremendous incitement"—i.e., due to his evil communion with the ghost of Quint, who, according to Mrs. Grose, was "so
clever, so deep." Seeing Miles and Flora strolling in the distance out of
earshot, the governess avers that they only "pretend to be lost in their
fairy-tale," which Miles is reading to his little sister; actually they are
"steeped in their vision of the dead restored. . . . He's not reading to
her . . . they're talking horrors!" From Mrs. Grose's point of view, and
ours too, it is the governess who is talking horrors—and nonsense as
well.

She finds the children delightfully, fascinatingly beautiful and good.
Does she enjoy these virtues in her charges? No, she pronounces their

beauty "more than earthly," their goodness "unnatural. . . . It's a game . . . it's a policy" and a fraud. Once more, we can only agree with her when she says to Mrs. Grose, "I go on, I know, as if I were crazy," and exclaims, after expounding her policy-and-fraud theory, "Yes, mad as that seems!" Exhausted by sleeplessness, she goes to bed at a reasonable hour, for once, leaving the candle burning. She awakes about 1:00 A.M. to find the light out. Aha, she feels "an instant certainty" that her beautiful little Flora has extinguished it. She cites "the systematic silence" of the children about Quint and Miss Jessel as the surest proof of the four's intercourse. It does not cross her mind that Miles and Flora may be silent about the pair because they know little or nothing to say about them.

Before leaving the governess to her cruel, unjustified inductions, one should scrutinize the atmosphere in which she arrives at them. Sometimes she is alone, and at such times she seems closest to the truth about herself. "Putting things at the worst . . . as in meditation I so often did" is a fairly accurate way of depicting her glum, solitary cerebrations. Alone again after Seizure 2, an hour of prostration, a hysterical parley with Mrs. Grose till after midnight, and no sleep, she has "restlessly read into the facts before us almost all the meaning they were to receive from subsequent . . . occurrences." The frankest of all her admissions in this vein comes after the nocturnal scare of surprising Miles on the lawn in the act (so she thinks) of communicating with Quint on the tower. It "was essentially in the scared state [induced by this episode] that I drew my actual conclusions." This confession alone is almost enough to brand as unsound all her conclusions achieved during moments of pronounced nervous instability.

She does not, decently, restrict her induction making and conclusion jumping to periods of solitude. Frighteningly, she carries them on while with Mrs. Grose. In fact, the housekeeper's presence acts as a stimulus, inciting the governess to wilder, more impetuous leaps than ever: "to put the thing with some coherence and with the mere aid of her presence to my own mind, I went on"—to declare Miles a pernicious influence on his schoolmates; "as she released me I made it out to

her, made it out perhaps only now with full coherency even to myself"
—that Flora had seen Miss Jessel's ghost but pretended not to; the
"very act of bringing it out [to Mrs. Grose] really helped me to trace it
—follow it all up and piece it all together."

There is something disquieting about the impulsive, improvisatory
tone of these remarks flung at Mrs. Grose as she rushes toward her
monstrous inductions. The tone may be heard again in the garbled,
jerky account of Seizure 2 with which the governess is furnishing Mrs.
Grose: "I quickly added stroke to stroke." Equally disquieting is the
note of hysteria often accompanying her improvisations, as when she
exclaims, "No, no—there are depths, depths! The more I go over it the
more I see in it, and the more I see in it the more I fear. I don't know
what I *don't* see, what I *don't* fear!"

This nescience is more honest than the alarming outburst that greets
Mrs. Grose when she impugns the accuracy of the governess' "identification" of Seizure 3. "But how do you know?" is Mrs. Grose's pertinent query. The governess' reply is fraught with hysteria (though she
prefers to call it "exaltation"): " 'I know, I know, I know!' My exaltation grew. 'And *you* know, my dear!' " As if repeating the phrase made
it so.

The nonapparitionist will already have caught the ironies embedded
in some of the quotations above, such as "made it out . . . with full coherency . . . to myself." These add one of the few notes of humor to
the desolate span of the governess' narrative, though the smiles provoked are wry rather than relaxed. To end the section on this note of
dubious cheer, here are other samples (italics ours):

A portentous clearness now possessed me.
"You do know, you dear thing [Mrs. Grose] . . . only you haven't *my
dreadful boldness of mind*, and you keep back, out of timidity and mod-
esty and delicacy, even the impression that in the past, when you had, *without my aid*, to flounder about in silence, most of all made you miserable."

"What I've seen . . . *has only made me more lucid*, made me get hold of
still other things."

My lucidity must have seemed awful.

The chain of my logic was ever too strong for her.

Poor Mrs. Grose. May the heavens preserve us all from exposure to such logic, lucidity, dreadful boldness, and portentous clearness as this.

◊◊◊◊◊◊◊◊◊◊◊◊◊◊◊◊◊◊◊◊◊◊◊◊◊◊

XII. *The Inquisitor and the Saint*

◊◊◊◊◊◊◊◊◊◊◊◊◊◊◊◊◊◊◊◊◊◊◊◊◊◊

THE NEXT facets of the governess' character to be examined involve her incomparable curiosity and her lust for martyrdom. Though her inquisitiveness has never been thoroughly studied or documented, we are not the first to notice it. In his introduction to *The Ghostly Tales,* Leon Edel writes of the "morbidly curious governess" that she is "curious to the point of exasperation; and it is a curiosity suppressed and never appeased." We agree with every word except "suppressed."

To say that the governess arrives at her inductions and jumps to her conclusions without first making a stab at canvassing the facts is unjust. She is in fact tireless in her researches. This is not to say that her methods of investigation are laudable. Despite her industry, she has serious failings as a researcher. For one thing, she is unwilling or unable to explore every possible source of information, depending for the most part on Mrs. Grose. Second, she does not collect her data systematically, and certainly not calmly, but piecemeal, frequently late at night when she has been unbalanced by insomnia, nervous exhaustion, and seizures. How can her way of evaluating what she collects be anything but a reflection of her own bents and biases, a method which the preceding section on the mystery of Miles's school partially illustrates?

Third, she fails to allow for the possible prejudices of her chief informant, Mrs. Grose. Next, she is seldom inclined to follow even the handful of facts she is able to garner to wherever they may logically lead, preferring to sort, rearrange, delete, augment, and otherwise misinterpret them to fit her own preconceived theories. Finally, the spirit in which she approaches her interrogations is heinous. It is the spirit of Torquemada, as exemplified in a few excerpts from her manuscript (italics ours):

> During the dialogue about Seizure 2 the governess thinks she finds in Mrs. Grose "the far-away faint glimmer of a consciousness more acute . . . the delayed dawn of an idea I myself had not given her and that was as yet quite obscure to me. . . . I thought instantly of this as something *I could get from her*."

> To "the victim of my confidence" the governess asserts, "the time has certainly come to give me the whole thing. . . . *I must have it now*."

> The governess seeks "further aid to intelligence" by *"pushing my colleague fairly to the wall."* Though Mrs. Grose has already told her, *"under pressure,* a great deal," the governess now feels "the importance of *giving the last jerk* to the curtain . . . *without sparing you the least bit more*—oh not a scrap, come!—*to get out of you."* Mrs. Grose is forced to elaborate a previous remark *"under my insistence."*

> "What she had said to him since *I pressed. . . . I pressed again,* of course, the closer for that."

> "Lord, *how I pressed* her now! . . . you keep back. . . . *But I shall get it out of you yet! . . . I persisted."*

> After suffering Seizure 6 (Miss Jessel in the schoolroom), the governess surmises that the children have bribed Mrs. Grose to silence, which she determines *"to break down* on the first private opportunity."

Note the consistent violence of the idiom in which her descriptions of the inquisitions are couched: "to get from," "to push to the wall," "to give to the curtain the last jerk," "to break down," and to "press, press, press," everlastingly "to press." As this voracious, insatiable, relentless questioner in place after place puts the screw to her victim, one wonders whether the sum total of mental agony produced is so very much less than what more notorious inquisitors inflicted upon their subjects.

The only imaginable defense apt to curry sympathy for the governess is that she is only reacting understandably to the pain James allots her as he kneads the mystifications thick. To cite two samples: before Miles arrives at Bly, she is so impatient to see him that she suffers "a curiosity that, all the next hours, was to deepen almost to pain"; and in the final scene she shakes the child as if to ask him why he had subjected her to months of "torment." The word is well chosen. Who can estimate the torment of the inquisitor condemned eternally to seek but not to find, usually because there is nothing to be found?

One need not expect that Mrs. Grose is often a cheerful deponent, but what is she to do? She adores the children and evidently never considers deserting them. She doesn't dare appeal to their uncle except possibly as a last resort. What she actually does is to make the best of the wretched state of affairs according to her lights, appearing one moment to submit to the vagaries of her superior, the governess in charge, the next moment trying to escape her, and occasionally attacking as well as defending herself from the questioner.

Here is a passage that tells much of Mrs. Grose's technique in the early stages of the story. When the governess first enunciates her cruel theory about Miles's school and her interview with the housekeeper is terminated, "the rest of the day, I watched for further occasion to approach my colleague, especially as, toward evening, I began to fancy she rather sought to avoid me. I overtook her . . . on the staircase; we went down together and at the bottom I detained her, holding her there with a hand on her arm." How unpleasant it must be to grow aware that the inquisitor is lying in wait, to be unable to escape her, to be trapped on the stairs, to feel the detaining hand—and then the inquisition starts.

In this particular scene the interrogated gives the interrogator as good as she gets. The governess writes, "She threw back her head; she had clearly, by this time, and very honestly, adopted an attitude." Subjected to a second spate of questions before the end of the same chapter, she says, "But please, Miss . . . I must get to my work." This fine exit line is followed by a sentence in which nonapparitionists descry a certain irony. According to the governess, Mrs. Grose's "thus turning her back on me was fortunately not . . . a snub that could check the growth of our mutual esteem." Mrs. Grose's technique on this occasion, in other words, proves ineffective, and the inquisitions, like the "esteem," continue to grow.

Even staying below stairs, where the governess, with her grand airs, seldom ventures, avails Mrs. Grose little. After Seizure 6 the governess is forced to descend to the housekeeper's room in order to secure at "the first private opportunity . . . five minutes with her," imposing her everlasting questions while Mrs. Grose sits "in pained placidity before the fire." Other intimations that Mrs. Grose tries to counter the grillings by making herself hard to find or by offering some sort of resistance, now passive, now active, are as follows: "As soon as I could compass a private word with Mrs. Grose . . ."; "[Mrs. Grose] had joined me, under pressure, on the terrace"; "My hand was on my friend's arm, but she failed for the moment . . . to respond to my pressure"; "my friend had discernibly now girded her loins to meet me afresh."

It is Mrs. Grose's unenviable lot to share the experiences of a young woman who has the earmarks of an inquisitor and some of the characteristics of a saint at the same time. The governess' intense desire to martyrize herself has not been lost on earlier readers. Robert Heilman discusses it, and John Lydenberg, following his lead, pronounces the governess "an almost classic case of what Erich Fromm calls the authoritarian character: masochistic in that she delights in receiving the tortures as an 'expiatory victim' . . . sadistic in her insistence on dominating the children and Mrs. Grose." There is no question that she talks and acts like some of the saints who were most avid for the halo, the palm, the wheel, and the griddle. What has not been sufficiently observed is that her lust for martyrdom is inseparable from her passion for the bachelor uncle. There are a number of passages that give her game away, of which two are fitting here:

She didn't know—no one knew—how proud I had been to serve him and to stick to our terms.

It was pleasure at these moments to feel myself tranquil and justified; doubtless perhaps also to reflect that by my discretion, my quiet good sense and general high propriety, I was giving pleasure—if he ever thought of it!— to the person to whose pressure I had yielded. What I was doing was what he had earnestly hoped and directly asked of me, and that I *could,* after all, do it proved even a greater joy than I had expected. I dare say I fancied myself in short a remarkable young woman and took comfort in the faith that this would more publicly appear. . . . Some one . . . would stand before me and smile and approve.

Sticking to one's bargain, shouldering the responsibilities, evincing quiet good sense, discretion, and high propriety are all very well, but what if these do not attract "publicly"—i.e., from the uncle—the gratitude, smiles, and approval for which she is starved? Harold C. Goddard expressed our views when he wrote:

When a young person, especially a young woman, falls in love and circumstances forbid the normal growth and confession of the passion, the emotion, dammed up, overflows in a psychical experience, a daydream, or internal drama. . . . In romantic natures this takes the form of imagined deeds of extraordinary heroism or self-sacrifice done in behalf of the beloved object. The governess' is precisely such a nature. . . . Her whole being tingles with the craving to perform some act of unexampled courage.

Apropos of Seizure 2, Goddard inquires:

Why has the stranger come for the children rather than for her? Because she must not merely be brave; she must be brave for someone's sake. The hero must be brought into the drama. She must save the beings whom he has commissioned her to protect. And that she may have the opportunity to save them they must be menaced: they must have enemies. That is the creative logic of her hallucination.

To this exposition we should add one further observation. What is more heroic than fighting off an evil spirit? Why, fighting off two evil spirits. Hence not only four seizures involving Enemy 1, Peter Quint, but four conjuring up Enemy 2, Miss Jessel. So much for "the fine machinery I had set in motion to attract his attention to my slighted charms," to employ the governess' own unflattering but in our view accurate way of summing up. As Katherine Anne Porter puts it, "She herself. . . . designed all this drama to make the desired situation possible—that she would arrive somewhere at a level with the man she loved and create some sort of communication with him."

Except for her comment on "the fine machinery"—and here she evidently intends to deliver herself of a shattering irony—the governess wastes little time analyzing the relation between seizures and passion, probably because she is so preoccupied with the details of the glorious martyrdom itself. But there is one other passage which indicates that the connection does not entirely elude her:

I was in these days literally able to find a joy in the extraordinary flight of heroism the occasion demanded of me. I now saw that I had been asked for a service admirable and difficult; and there would be a greatness in letting it be seen—oh in the right quarter!—that I could succeed where many another girl might have failed. It was an immense help to me—I confess I rather applaud myself as I look back!—that I saw my response so strongly and so simply. I was there to protect and defend the little creatures in the world the most bereaved and the most loveable, the appeal of whose helplessness had suddenly become only too explicit, a deep constant ache of one's own engaged affection. We were cut off, really, together; we were united in our danger. They had nothing but me, and I—well, I had *them*. It was in short a magnificent chance. This chance presented itself to me in an image richly material. I was a screen—I was to stand before them. The more I saw the less they would.

To "find a joy in the extraordinary flight of heroism," "a greatness in letting it be seen . . . in the right quarter," it was "a magnificent chance"—the phrases are a dead give-away. St. Praxed in a Glory could not have been more ecstatic.

After Seizure 2 she gives another comprehensive commentary on the matter. "I had an absolute certainty that I should see again what I had already seen, but something within me said that by offering myself bravely as the sole object of such experience, by accepting, by inviting, by surmounting it all, I should serve as an expiatory victim and guard the tranquillity of the rest of the household. The children in especial I should thus fence about and absolutely save."

Such citations could be continued almost indefinitely, but a few more will do to show how ubiquitous is this attitude throughout. "I knew at this hour, I think, as well as I knew later, what I was capable of meeting to shelter my pupils." It "would from that moment distress me much more to lose my power [of receiving ghostly visitations] than to keep it. . . . I greatly preferred, as a safeguard, the fulness of my own exposure." Let us not forget what Quint's face at the window produces in her, "the most extraordinary effect . . . a sudden vibration of duty and courage," so that she bounds straight out of the house in pursuit of her foe.

James may have derived the title of his story from a passage in his own text, a passage, it so happens, that concerns the governess' martyrdom and her attitude toward it. If so, the quotation affords an index to how important the author considered this facet of her character: "I could only get on at all . . . by treating my monstrous ordeal as a push in a direction unusual, of course, and unpleasant, but demanding, after all, for a fair front, only another turn of the screw of ordinary human virtue." Could any indication be clearer that she now considers herself among the company set apart by extraordinary displays of virtue—the company of the saints?

A clue to the depth of this craving for martyrdom can be seen in her reactions when the palm is in danger of slipping from her grasp. After listening to Miles play the piano for a time which she has ceased to measure, "I started up with a strange sense of having literally slept at my post." How interesting the military trope is. Does she temporarily fancy herself as Joan of Arc? Again, after Seizure 3, bursting into tears, " 'I don't do it!' I sobbed in despair; 'I don't save or shield them! It's far worse than I dreamed. They're lost!' "

As an antidote to this unwonted burst of weakness, let us view the governess in a more characteristic mood, "professing that my personal exposure had suddenly become the least of my discomforts" and proclaiming her martyrdom complete during Seizure 4 since "dread had unmistakeably quitted me and . . . there was nothing in me unable to meet and measure." Somehow, in this mood she seems more attractive than when those momentary but fortunately infrequent uncertainties about her sainthood assail her. Personally, we dislike her least when she is trudging resolutely upwards to her own curious Zion.

Goddard's analysis of "the creative logic" behind her heroism and hallucinations makes nonapparitionists ponder the motivation behind one of the latter. Before Seizure 6 (Chapter XV) she determines to quit Bly—and her quest for Zion. She goes home to pack and proceeds as far as the schoolroom to collect her belongings there. Then she interrupts her preparations to indulge in her encounter with Miss Jessel, which leaves her with "a sense that I must stay." Why a seizure at the very moment her conscious mind has prompted her at last to decisive action? Because wild horses cannot drag her from her martyrdom—and from the chance of another meeting with the man she loves. Couched in psychological terms, the explanation might run as follows. To counter the conscious decision to flee, the governess' subconscious mind conjures up the seizure which makes flight impossible. Her heroism challenged, she brings herself round to the same old attitude to which she clings. And so the saint goes marching on.

XIII. *Some Bothersome Questions*

IN "The Ambiguity of Henry James," Edmund Wilson admits that there are "points in the story which are difficult to explain on this [nonapparitionist] theory," an admission which the late Wolcott Gibbs echoes in saying that the nonapparitionist "explanation of the author's intention leaves some bothersome questions to be answered . . . but on the whole it seems to me far more tenable than any supernatural hypothesis." Yvor Winters also notices "a few small difficulties of interpretation either way"—whether the story receives an apparitionist or nonapparitionist reading—though he himself finds Wilson's "hypothesis . . . more plausible than the popular one."

One of the bothersome questions grows out of the curious episode recounted in Chapters X and XI. The bare facts, insofar as they can be extricated from the governess' excited prose, are these. The governess awakens about one in the morning and sits up, completely aroused. The candle she has left burning is out. Flora, behind the blind and peering out the window, seems undisturbed by the governess' lighting the candle, donning slippers and wrap, and going out of the room into the corridor. Intending to go to some other window in the same quarter, the governess pauses in the hall, listens at Miles's door, and hears nothing. She descends to a lower room, looks out the window, and sees a person some distance away on the lawn. She hurries to meet this figure, and presently makes it out to be Miles. He immediately comes to her on the terrace. Wordless, she takes him upstairs to his room, where she sinks upon the edge of his bed, which has not been slept in, and demands from him "all the truth," why he went out and what he was doing. He explains that the whole thing has been a prank designed to make the governess think him bad for a change. He and Flora have devised for Flora to rise, look out the window, and disturb the governess so that she would surprise him.

Now for the governess' interpretation of the episode. Upon awakening she feels instantly sure that Flora has blown the candle out. When Flora does not emerge from behind the blind and gives no sign of being disturbed by the governess' putting on her things, the governess believes this lack of reaction constitutes proof that the child is now absorbed in communication with Miss Jessel. In the hall she announces to herself that there is "a figure in the grounds—a figure prowling for a sight, the visitor with whom Flora was engaged; but it wasn't the visitor most concerned with my boy." When she descries through the window the figure on the lawn "motionless . . . as if fascinated," though it is "diminished by distance" she states positively that it is looking "not so much straight at me as at something . . . clearly another person above me . . . a person on the tower." With a courage she has displayed at least once before in similar circumstances, she hurries out to meet the "presence," which she shortly makes out to be Miles.

Upon fetching him upstairs to his room, she is unequal to accusing him of doing what she is convinced he has actually been doing and ostensibly accepts his explanation of the prank, "exactly the account of himself that permitted least my going behind it." But no compunctions deter her the next morning from deluging Mrs. Grose with her bizarre interpretation of the events. She avers that Miles, Flora, Quint, and Miss Jessel perpetually meet; that the children "haven't been good —they've only been absent . . . they're simply leading a life of their own. They're not mine—they're not ours. They're his and they're hers!"

While apparitionists are prepared to believe her unreservedly, others prefer to seek different explanations. Katherine Anne Porter has taken especial note of the bright moonlight upon which James dwells during the episode. There is "a great still moon"; it makes "the night extraordinarily penetrable"; the governess emerges from the house into the moonlight, which makes Miles's room, to which they eventually repair, "so clear" that she doesn't need to light a candle. Probably as a consequence of all this reiterated moonshine, Miss Porter writes, "the governess persistently tries to fix upon the children evil motives and base actions. . . . their simplest and most natural acts are interpreted by the governess as being of a suspicious nature, even when they got up in the night and went out to look at the moonlight."

Sensitive and perceptive though Miss Porter is as a critic, we personally prefer Harold C. Goddard's suggestions. Of the moonlit episode he writes,

The scene is not narrated this time; it is presented—but only indirectly. The governess, looking down from a window, catches Miles out at midnight on the lawn. He gazes up, as nearly as she can figure, to a point on the building over her head. Whereupon she promptly draws the inference. "There was clearly another person above me—there was a person on the tower." This, when we stop to think, is even "thinner" than in the case of Flora and Miss Jessel, for this time even the governess does not see, she merely infers. The boy gazes up. "Clearly" there was a man upon the tower. That "clearly" lets the cat out of the bag. It shows, as every tyro in psychology should know, that "clear" is precisely what the thing is not.

How completely innocent and natural the children really were through all these earlier passages of the drama anyone will see who will divest himself of the suggestion that the governess has planted in his mind. The pranks they play are utterly harmless, and when she questions the perpetrators, because they are perfectly truthful, they have the readiest and most convincing answers at hand. Why did little Miles get up in the middle of the night and parade out on the lawn? Just as he said, in order that, for once, she might think him *bad*. Why did Flora rise from her bed at the same hour? By agreement with Miles. Why did she gaze out the window? To disturb her governess and make her look too. These answers, true every one, ought to have disarmed the children's inquisitor. But she has her satanic hypothesis, so that the very readiness of their replies convicts instead of acquitting them in her eyes. They are inspired answers, she holds, splendidly but diabolically inspired. They scintillate with a mental power beyond the children's years.

Though this reading of the incident is both credible and charitable, it by no means exhausts the theories which could be advanced. For one thing, the context of the episode may be significant. It occurs after Seizure 4 and its remarkable consequences. Returning to her room from her confrontation of Quint on the stairs, the governess finds Flora behind the blind and behaves in a markedly hysterical manner. She drops into her chair, feels faint, closes her eyes, questions the child, stares at her, "in the state of my nerves" believes absolutely that she is lying, grips "my little girl with a spasm," springs to her feet, and ends the session "by almost sitting on her for the retention of her hand."

It would be hard to imagine a less restful roommate for an eight-year-old girl. Seizure 5 (Miss Jessel on the stairs) follows hard on the heels of Seizure 4. The governess repeatedly sits up till she doesn't know when, selects moments when Flora is "unmistakeably" asleep, and takes "noiseless turns" in the passage. This goes on for ten nights straight running. Miles descends to the lawn on the eleventh night, the first of many when she has retired unusually early and slept for a few hours. That Flora has "unmistakeably" slept during all these excursions is doubtful; that the governess' "noiseless turns" in the hall are less noiseless than she supposes will be proved in a subsequent section.

In short, the children of course know of her strange nocturnal doings. Do they take the first chance they have, when she is finally sleeping for a change, to investigate for themselves? Or are they giving her an object lesson? Like the governess, on the eleventh night Miles has sat up till midnight reading, he says, then gone prowling. To disturb her rest as she has so often disturbed theirs? Or perhaps he has gone down to confer with Mrs. Grose, whom he has few opportunities to consult alone, learned from her of the suppositious visitor on the tower, and gone to the lawn to see for himself.

As support for the latter theory one could cite a passage in Chapter XIV. Strolling with the governess to church, Miles treats her to three speeches, the essence of which is "you can't say I've not been awfully good, can you? . . . Except just that one night, you know . . . when I went down—went out of the house." The dash is eloquent. What was he about to say before he caught himself and revised the sentence? Since the governess haughtily makes clear more than once the location of Mrs. Grose's quarters "below stairs," one immediately thinks of one plausible ending to the statement: "except just that one night . . . when I went downstairs to tell Mrs. Grose how disturbed our nights had been and ask her advice."

At this stage of the novel, incidentally, Flora's lot is less enviable than Miles's. She has to occupy the same room with the sleepless, prowling one. James takes pains to underscore the closeness and affection of the children. Miles's love for Flora is everywhere evident, and Flora adores her big brother. When the governess witlessly asks Miles, "Don't you then *love* our sweet Flora," he replies, "If I didn't—and you too; if I didn't—!" One of the most affecting scenes in the story, on the morning after Miles takes to the lawn, shows the children strolling on the lawn while the governess and Mrs. Grose watch from a distance "the charming creatures . . . in their interlocked sweetness" as Miles reads to his sister. He has his arm around her "to keep her quite in touch." His attitude toward her here and elsewhere is protective.

Bearing this relationship in mind, reread Miles's answer to the governess' question, "What did you go out for?" He replies, "just exactly in order that you should do this . . . . think me—for a change—*bad*!" What if the governess has not fully indicated the cadence of Miles's words and the emphasis belongs on "me" as well as on "bad"? The sense of his speech would then be "I prowled around so that you might think *me*—for a change—*bad*!" The boy may be trying to divert the governess' attention from Flora to himself and thus relieve the little girl trapped in that restless bedroom. The possibility is a poignant one.

In alluding to the bothersome questions in *The Turn of the Screw*, the three professed nonapparitionists Edmund Wilson, Yvor Winters, and Wolcott Gibbs have in mind primarily Mrs. Grose's "identification" of Quint, which is cited with firm reiteration by apparitionists as proof positive that from the governess' detailed description of the figure on the tower and the face at the window a woman who knew the valet in life is now able confidently to identify the image as his.

A good many nonapparitionists think not. Oscar Cargill suggests that the admittedly arresting details of Quint's appearance "must have come . . . from the prattle of her youngest charge," for, on the governess' second day at Bly, Flora has shown her the place "room by room and secret by secret," displaying a "disposition to tell me so many more things than she asked."

John Silver's study of the text has persuaded him that after Seizure 1 the governess has ample opportunity to repair to the neighboring village, only twenty minutes away from Bly "through the park and by the good road," where she could learn both how Quint looked and the whole story of his death. With this explanation Edmund Wilson expresses agreement in a note appended to "The Ambiguity of Henry James," reprinted in Gerald Willen's *Casebook*: "As for the explanation of the governess's describing correctly the person of Peter Quint, it is so clear—though slily contrived—one wonders how one could ever have missed it; yet it has never, so far as I know, been brought out before the publication . . . of a paper by John Silver."

Goddard observes that before presenting her circumstantial description, the governess has made the apparition out vaguely to be a horror in human form who is a threat to Miles and Flora. Goddard proposes that this is enough to set Mrs. Grose to thinking of Quint and that when further details come Mrs. Grose's identification rests on not all but only some of them. As usual, we are inclined toward Goddard's views, for a number of reasons. Since the apparitionists make so much of the scene of "identification," a close analysis of it from the other point of view seems in order.

To recapitulate briefly, when the governess thinks she sees Quint's evil face at the window, she does not, sanely, call for help or flee. On the contrary, the saint and martyr of Bly, blazing with a sense of duty and courage, charges from the room, out of the house, and along the terrace. She sees nothing, not even Quint in flight. She infers, irrationally, that he is not behind the shrubberies or big trees. Now it is "confusedly present" to her that she should stand where he stood and look through the window into the room she has just left. She scares the wits out of Mrs. Grose, who enters the dining room, sees the governess, turns white, stares, and hurries outside to meet her. Chapter IV, much of which James fills with this episode, ends as Mrs. Grose rushes to the governess' side. The governess' last sentence in the chapter is the wildly ironic "I wondered why *she* should be scared."

The women's subsequent interview, including the famous description of Quint, James dramatically allots a chapter of its own. Whatever one may think of this description and Mrs. Grose's "identification," they are certainly not prompt in coming. In fact, the next development reminds one of a passage in James Thurber's "The Macbeth Murder Case," in which a skeptical woman reader nominates Macduff as the principal suspect in Duncan's murder because Macduff rushes from the king's chamber and cries,

> Confusion now hath made his masterpiece!
> Most sacrilegious murther hath broke ope
> The Lord's anointed temple and stole thence
> The life o' th' building!

The woman pounces on this speech as extremely odd: "People don't just say things like that on the spur of the moment. They say, 'My God, there's a dead body in there'." She would have pounced also on the governess' words and deeds at this moment. Instead of running to meet Mrs. Grose with "My God, I've just seen a man glaring in the window," she stands her ground while Mrs. Grose, flushed and breathless, rounds the corner and cries "What in the name of goodness is the matter—?"

The governess gives no reply to this query until Mrs. Grose comes "quite near," and when the reply comes, it is rambling and deranged. Here is the exchange between the two women, divested of the governess' dubious interpretations of Mrs. Grose's looks and words and presented, again, like dialogue from a play. The bracketed queries are ours.

Mrs. Grose. What in the name of goodness is the matter—?
The Governess (making "a wonderful face"). With me? Do I show it?
Mrs. Grose. You're as white as a sheet. You look awful.
The Governess (wavering, putting out her hand for Mrs. Grose to take). You came for me for church, of course, but I can't go.
Mrs. Grose. Has anything happened?
The Governess. Yes. You must know now. Did I look very queer?
Mrs. Grose. Through this window? Dreadful!
The Governess. Well, I've been frightened. Just what you saw from the dining-room a minute ago was the effect of that. What *I* saw—just before —was much worse.
Mrs. Grose (tightening her grip on the governess' hand). What was it?
The Governess. An extraordinary man. Looking in.
Mrs. Grose. What extraordinary man?
The Governess. I haven't the least idea.
Mrs. Grose (gazing vainly about). Then where is he gone?
The Governess. I know still less.
Mrs. Grose. Have you seen him before?
The Governess. Yes—once. On the old tower.
Mrs. Grose (looking at her harder). Do you mean he's a stranger?
The Governess. Oh very much!
Mrs. Grose. Yet you didn't tell me?
The Governess. No—for reasons [i.e., for fear you'd think me mad?]. But now that you've guessed [that I have "spells"?]—
Mrs. Grose (round-eyed). Ah I haven't guessed! How can I if *you* don't imagine?
The Governess. I don't in the very least.
Mrs. Grose. You've seen him nowhere but on the tower?
The Governess. And on this spot just now.
Mrs. Grose (surveying the grounds again). What was he doing on the tower?
The Governess. Only standing there and looking down at me.
Mrs. Grose [suspecting, after a moment's thought, that she has "seen" the master?]. Was he a gentleman?
The Governess (finding that she has no need to think). No. (Mrs. Grose gazes in deeper wonder.) No.

Mrs. Grose. Then nobody about the place? Nobody from the village?

The Governess. Nobody—nobody. I didn't tell you, but I made sure.

Mrs. Grose (breathing vague relief). But if he isn't a gentleman—

The Governess. What *is* he? He's a horror.

Mrs. Grose. A horror?

The Governess. He's—God help me if I know *what* he is [i.e., if I know whether he's a real man or a figment of my imagination?]!

Mrs. Grose (looking round again, then pulling herself together and turning to the governess "with full inconsequence"). It's time we should be at church. [She has decided the governess *has* been "imagining things" and wants to dismiss the subject?]

The Governess. Oh, I'm not fit for church!

Mrs. Grose. Won't it do you good?

The Governess (nodding at the house). It won't do *them*—!

Mrs. Grose. The children?

The Governess. I can't leave them now.

Mrs. Grose. You're afraid—?

The Governess (boldly). I'm afraid of *him*.

Mrs. Grose. When was it [why not *he*? Because she regards "it" as a product of the governess' imagination?]—on the tower?

The Governess. About the middle of the month. At this same hour.

Mrs. Grose. Almost at dark [i.e., the likeliest time for you to imagine that you saw someone?].

The Governess. Oh no, not nearly. I saw him as I see you.

Mrs. Grose. Then how did he get in?

The Governess. And how did he get out? (She laughs [hysterically?].) I had no opportunity to ask him! This evening, you see, he has not been able to get in.

Mrs. Grose. He only peeps?

The Governess. I hope it will be confined to that! (Mrs. Grose has now released her hand and turned away [again incredulous and wanting to dismiss the subject?]. The governess pauses an instant.) Go to church. Good-bye. I must watch [spoken dramatically and calculated to detain Mrs. Grose further?].

Mrs. Grose (slowly facing her). Do you fear for them?

The Governess (meeting her "in another long look"). Don't *you*? (Mrs. Grose does not answer, but puts her face to the window.) You see how he could see.

Mrs. Grose. How long was he here?

The Governess. Till I came out. I came to meet him.

Mrs. Grose [noting the irrationality of this reaction?]. *I* couldn't have come out.

The Governess. Neither could I! (She laughs again.) But I did come. I've my duty.

Mrs. Grose. So have I mine [i.e., to determine whether the children's governess is demented and if so to protect them against her?] What's he like?

The Governess. I've been dying to tell you [laughable, in view of her almost interminable delay in doing so?]. But he's like nobody.

Mrs. Grose. Nobody?

The Governess. He has no hat.

What a strange place to begin one's description of a horror who's like nobody. The most ardent apparitionist must grant that the governess' lines may be read as disjointed, irrational, hysterical outpourings. How long she takes in coming to any specific, meaningful descriptive details at all. Between the time Mrs. Grose heaves into sight at the beginning of Chapter V and at last receives the breathtaking news that the intruder wears no hat, the governess uses up 867 words in her narrative.

The bit about the hat, however, is the beginning of the detailed description. The hatlessness visibly impresses Mrs. Grose, who "with a deeper dismay," finds in it "a touch of picture" and so encourages the governess to supply at last the particulars which she has delayed giving for so long.

He has no hat. . . . He has red hair, very red, close-curling, and a pale face, long in shape, with straight good features and little rather queer whiskers that are as red as his hair. His eyebrows are somewhat darker; they look particularly arched and as if they might move a good deal. His eyes are sharp, strange—awfully; but I only know clearly that they're rather small and very fixed. His mouth's wide, and his lips are thin, and except for his little whiskers he's quite clean-shaven. He gives me a sort of sense of looking like an actor. . . . I've never seen one, but so I suppose them. He's tall, active, erect . . . but never—no, never!—a gentleman.

Mrs. Grose, it now appears, believes in ghosts too, for the moment at least. After three questions she identifies the governess' apparition for her—and thus does her a vast disservice. After the governess' emphatic

judgment about the apparition's lack of gentility, Mrs. Grose scorn-
fully asks, a "gentleman *he?*" Her second question is "But he *is* handsome?" The governess sees "the way to help her" and replies, "Remarkably!" The third question: "And dressed—?" to which the governess replies "In somebody's clothes. They're smart, but they're not his
own." The housekeeper groans, "They're the master's," and completes
her identification: "Peter Quint—his own man, his valet, when he was
here! . . . He never wore his hat, but he did wear—well, there were
waistcoats missed! They were both here—last year. Then the master
went, and Quint was alone. . . . Alone with *us*. . . . In charge." Finally
she tells the governess that Quint is dead.

There are several peculiarities about the housekeeper's identification.
Observe that while the governess raves for three pages about the apparition before collecting herself sufficiently to describe it, Mrs. Grose, obviously incredulous, interrupts with questions like a prosecuting attor-
ney and apparently tries twice to deflect the governess from further discussion. What finally convinces her that the governess has indeed seen
a ghost and that the ghost is Quint? The ghost wears no hat, he is de-
cidedly not a gentleman, he is handsome, he looks like an actor and is
therefore not dressed in his own clothes. She offers no comment and
asks no questions about the long, pale face, the red hair and whiskers,
the dark, arched, mobile eyebrows, the small, sharp, strange eyes, the
wide mouth, the thin lips, the tall stature, the erectness of figure. But
she knew Quint: he was handsome, but no gentleman. The ghost is
handsome, but no gentleman. Quint wore—"well, there were waistcoats missed," so Quint must have "borrowed" or stolen them and
worn them. The ghost is dressed "In somebody's clothes." That somebody could only be the master. Quint did not, however, wear the
master's hat. The ghost wears no hat. Ergo, the ghost is Quint.

How this evidence, upon which Mrs. Grose mainly bases her identification, would impress a court of law one may easily surmise. Being hat-
less, handsome, no gentleman, and dressed in another's clothes are
points too lacking in concreteness to permit a positive identification,

legal or otherwise. Goddard emphasizes their flimsiness by drawing an analogy:

Suppose a missing criminal is described as follows: "A squat, ruddy-cheeked man about thirty years old, weighing nearly two hundred pounds; thick lips and pockmarked face; one front tooth missing, two others with heavy gold fillings; big scar above left cheek bone. Wears shell glasses; had on, when last seen, brown suit, gray hat, pink shirt and tan shoes." Then suppose a man, flushed with excitement, were to rush into police headquarters exclaiming that he had found the murderer. "How do you know?" the chief detective asks. "Why! I saw a man about thirty years old with shell glasses and tan shoes!"

Well, it is only a slight exaggeration to say that Mrs. Grose's "identification" of Peter Quint, in the face of the governess' description, is of exactly this sort.

One wonders to what extent Mrs. Grose is led to her identification by her attitude toward Quint: "a gentleman *he?*" she scathingly asks. Certainly not; yet last year he was left alone at Bly "with us" and in charge! When the governess asks where Quint has gone, Mrs. Grose, with an extraordinary expression, cries, "God knows where! He died." It soon appears, however, that if God doesn't know, Mrs. Grose does: he is in hell. Alive, he has provoked in her such grave disapproval and bitter resentment that now she brings herself, and the governess along with her, to believe, temporarily, at least, that he continues though dead to plague the household. How profound her loathing and fear of the live Quint must have been to force her to such a belief!

Since the governess' conception of Quint depends on Mrs. Grose's, the latter's deserves further study. Why does she disapprove of Quint, apart from the missing waistcoats? In several widely scattered places throughout the novel she gives to the governess, usually under duress, many details. These and Mrs. Grose's picture of the dead man in general are matter for another section.

XIV. *I Know My Place*

JAMES took a lively interest in the English caste system of which he was both a part and an observer for most of his life. In *The Real Thing*, published six years before *The Turn of the Screw*, James conveyed some of his chief ideas about art; but the story also tells much about class and its effects on the British, for it concerns a faded, impoverished major and his wife who are bested at modeling for an artist by "a common, clever, London girl, of the smallest origin" and by a professional Italian smelling of garlic (*Notebooks*, p. 104). In lieu of the gentry in *The Real Thing* with their well-bred, "everlasting English amateurishness," each reader, drawing from his own favorite story or novel, could doubtless supply his favorite instances of James's patent sensitivity to the social hierarchy.

In his notebooks, to cite one further example, James wrote on October 18, 1895, in Torquay, two years before he dictated *The Turn of the Screw,*

The idea of the picture, fully satiric, in illustration of the "Moloch-worship" of the social hierarchy in this country—the grades and shelves and stages of relative gentility—the image of some succession or ladder of examples, in which each state, each "party," has something or someone below them, down to extreme depths, on which, on whom, the snubbed and despised from above, may wreak resentment by doing, below, as they are done by. They have to take it from Peter, but they give it to Paul. Follow the little, long, close series—the tall column of Peters and Pauls.

James never wrote this story precisely as outlined, but there are distinct reflections of it in *The Turn of the Screw*. It seems to us that James often sounds this note at Bly—harps on it, in fact. Yet critics have hitherto virtually turned a deaf ear to it, overlooking a significant theme vital to a nice appreciation of the story.

First for that principal character in the dramatis personae, the governess. Only Margaret Marshall seems to have noted that she "is obsessed with class distinctions, and the part this obsession plays in the story is fascinating." As victims of genteel poverty often are, the governess is inordinately aware of the only possession which sets her apart from the ruck and run—her gentility. She and Miles and Flora are the only gentle folk at Bly; and over them and the entire household, she has been assured by her employer, she is to be "in supreme authority." Much has been written about this authority, by James himself and by both apparitionists and nonapparitionists. In his preface James says, "She has 'authority,' which is a good deal to have given her." To quote Oliver Evans's apparitionist reaction to this statement, James does not mean authority "where the *children* are concerned, but where the *reader* is."

Surely her account of the doings at Bly must in a sense be judged uniquely authoritative since it is the only account we have. But unless she does indeed have authority over the children and the servants, how is one to explain the passage in the prologue in which the trustworthy Douglas, conveying information he has obtained from the governess' own lips, says, "There were plenty of people to help [at Bly], but of course the young lady who should go down as governess would be in supreme authority"? After this pointed definition of the position which the governess accepts, it seems fruitless to insist that she is a governess who is not expected to govern.

Certainly the governess herself is in no doubt about her powers, once she is established at Bly. Enroute to the estate, she confesses she has "rather brooded" over her "relation" with Mrs. Grose, the relation between a twenty-year-old newcomer of gentle birth and no experience who is to be in charge of a corps of servants, and a middle-aged, experienced housekeeper who before the governess' arrival has been "acting for the time as superintendent to the little girl, of whom, without children of her own, she was by good luck extremely fond." But Mrs. Grose immediately dispels the governess' apprehension by meeting her at the door with Flora and dropping her "as decent a curtsey as if I had been the mistress or a distinguished visitor"; "from the first moment," then, she feels assured that "I shall get on with Mrs. Grose."

Oh, the governess is in charge, all right, and moreover exceedingly jealous of her authority. When she invokes her first apparition and is ignorant of its identity, she bridles "with the sense of how my office seemed to require that there should be no such ignorance and no such person." Her office! When she first sees the female apparition, she sees "an alien object in view—a figure whose right of presence I instantly and passionately questioned." When Mrs. Grose tells her that Quint was too free with Miles, the governess exclaims, "Too free with *my* boy?" Authority, you see, breeds possessiveness. The bookish may recall, in this connection, many a lady librarian who eventually comes to regard the volumes she tends as her personal property, not lightly to be lent, or fetched, to every Tom, Dick, and Harry.

Also noteworthy is the patronizing air of many of the governess' references to Mrs. Grose. To the governess, the housekeeper seems "a civil person," a "stout simple plain clean wholesome woman." When made "a receptacle of lurid things" by the governess, Mrs. Grose shows "an odd recognition of my superiority—my accomplishments and my function." But *noblesse oblige*: the governess feels "that I doubtless needn't press too hard, in such company [Mrs. Grose's], on the place of a servant in the scale." Nevertheless, at one point, the governess can say to her, "If Quint . . . was a base menial, one of the things Miles said to you, I find myself guessing, was that you were another." It is no wonder that after many such ladylike remarks Mrs. Grose's eyes express "plainly" that she knows "too well her place not to be ready to share with me any marked inconvenience." Even among the Victorians, it seems, there were those who were gratified to find a servant who knew her place. Let us hope that the governess takes some of the edge off her frequently haughty attitude when she embraces and kisses "the good creature," Mrs. Grose.

Near the end of the tale, when the governess is almost at the end of her tether, it is significant that she reacts to her difficulties by suffering a severe attack of the haughties. To avoid "total wreck" she clutches "the helm," and "to bear up at all" becomes "very grand and very dry," while "the aspect of others" shows "a confused reflexion of the crisis." Their gaping and staring only further exacerbate her nerves, so that she causes it to be known that, left to herself, she is "quite remarkably firm." Were she a man, she might thrust her hand into her bosom and become Napoleon in grand, solitary state upon Elba. As it is, she looks, "I have no doubt, as if I were ready for any onset." And so "with that manner" she wanders "for the next hour or two, all over the place." She "parades." Then to "mark, for the house, the high state" which she is cultivating, she "decrees" that her meals with Miles are to be served "downstairs . . . in the ponderous pomp of the [dining] room." Here is hauteur indeed. It would not come as a very great shock to hear her cry, over dinner, "Off with their heads!" Too acute an appreciation of one's station in life as a lady and governess in supreme authority can be very unsettling, especially when that authority is about to evaporate.

The fanciful might wonder why Mrs. Grose, when besieged by all this grandeur, does not rebel. How can she resist declaring, in her own words, what Viola declares to Olivia, "I see you what you are—you are too proud"? The answer is that it never occurs to the housekeeper to question the validity of the system to which she is bound. Does she not find it right and fitting, subscribe to it as readily, as automatically, as the governess herself? To put it another way, is not Mrs. Grose as big a snob as the governess? Let us review what James would call Mrs. Grose's grade, shelf, stage, or rung of the ladder in the social scale.

In the prologue her station is defined with some care. The uncle of Miles and Flora "had put them in possession of Bly . . . and had placed at the head of their little establishment—but belowstairs only—an excellent woman, Mrs. Grose . . . who had formerly been maid to his mother. She was now housekeeper and was also acting for the time as suprintendent to the little girl." Since the death of Miss Jessel, the governess' predecessor, "Mrs. Grose . . . in the way of manners and things, had done as she could for Flora." An excellent woman, formerly a lady's maid, whilom head of the household, childless, temporarily superintendent of Flora, of whom she is extremely fond and whose "manners and things" she oversees—not a poor lot for an unlettered woman.

But not to be missed is the pregnant phrase *belowstairs only*. It is this part of James's definition of her station that her language and deportment very frequently recall. Apart from the decent curtsy with which she welcomes the governess and the other abundant references in the governess' manuscript to Mrs. Grose's social subservience, notice how scrupulous she is in addressing or referring to the gentry in her little world. To her the governess is always Miss, while Miles and Flora are invariably Miss Flora, Master Miles, the little lady, the young gentleman, and the like. The fact that she is unable to read or write does not mean, obviously, that she is incapable of verbally observing a certain etiquette. Exactly what she does for Flora "in the way of manners and things" James never specifies, but one of our first guesses is that in the little girl she inculcates some of these same social niceties to which she seems throughout to be sensitive.

The questions Mrs. Grose asks about Seizure 1 (Quint on the tower) follow an interesting order. After asking sensibly why the governess had not informed her of the experience, Mrs. Grose inquires whether he had appeared anywhere else and what he was doing on the tower. Then the climactic question: "Was he a gentleman?" And so Mrs. Grose again sounds the note which rings throughout the rest of the scene. Let us examine only those portions relevant to our inquiry into Mrs. Grose's picture of the social hierarchy and her own niche in it.

Review her judgment of Peter Quint: "A gentleman? . . . a gentleman *he*?" Certainly not. Yet "Alone with *us*." And "In charge." Why
did the arrangement fill Mrs. Grose with loathing and fear? Because
Quint was no gentleman and therefore was unqualified to rule the
roost? Because Quint was evil in addition to lacking gentility? Because
her own station at Bly was threatened or rendered equivocal by Quint's
presence? Mrs. Grose's attitude could be due to any or all of these.
Happily, there is further evidence to explain the antagonistic, bristling
posture that mention of Quint invariably prompts Mrs. Grose to adopt.

First, the question of who was in charge of what and whom at Bly,
in what order. Here the chronology of the authority exercised is confused. According to the prologue, the uncle confides in the governess,
"It had all been a great worry and, on his part doubtless, a series of
blunders." Could one of the blunders have been not delegating power
and defining authority with sufficient clarity? He had become the children's guardian two years before his interview with the governess and
had sent them to Bly "from the first . . . parting even with his own servants to wait on them," including his valet, Quint, and Mrs. Grose,
formerly his mother's maid. He had placed the latter at the head of
their little establishment, though belowstairs only. But also "at first"
there had been Miss Jessel, who "had done for them quite beautifully"
as governess; and in addition at one stage of the game Quint was left
alone in charge. With Mrs. Grose, Miss Jessel, and Peter Quint—all
three of them—on the scene, one begins to suspect that Bly might have
been ripe for what labor circles call jurisdictional disputes. Was the
master seeking to avoid a repetition of a blunder when he made it ever
so clear that the *next* "young lady who should go down as governess
would be in supreme authority"?

What of the social ladder at Bly during these confusing years? Who
belonged, literally and figuratively, above, who below, stairs? Any who
are inclined to dismiss such a query as trifling or inapposite might reread *The Admirable Crichton* or Henry Green's *Loving*; or they might
recollect the intricacies of the British system of domestic economy in
the Good Old Days, when there was a variety of maids, beginning with

Milady's Own and descending to the Upstairs and Downstairs, separated by Tweenies—and by who knows what social distinctions which they themselves found meaningful. At any rate, that at least one of the dwellers at Bly remained acutely conscious of such distinctions is proved by further testimony from Mrs. Grose.

Grilled repeatedly by the governess, the housekeeper surrenders some interesting information. The following dialogue is divested of the governess' ruminations and interpretations:

The Governess. And you tell me they [Quint and Miles] were "great friends"?

Mrs. Grose. Oh it wasn't *him* [Miles]. It was Quint's own fancy. To play with him, I mean—to spoil him. Quint was much too free.

The Governess. Too free with *my* boy?

Mrs. Grose. Too free with every one!

This brief excerpt raises a semantic problem that revolves about the word *free*. One of its definitions, according to *The New English Dictionary,* in part reads, "in bad sense—overfree, forward, 'familiar,' ready to 'take liberties'." This fits well enough the impression of Quint so far gained from Mrs. Grose. But the *NED* offers yet another meaning: "Not observing due bounds, 'loose,' licentious." Apparently impressed by the latter meaning and several additional passages, some critics—G. C. Knight, F. R. Leavis, and Joseph J. Firebaugh, for example—detect in such dialogue hints of a homosexual relationship between the valet and the boy. That Mrs. Grose has in mind sexual rather than social liberties is exceedingly hard to prove, however.

On the other hand, it is quite easy to prove that, whatever else she may be thinking of, Mrs. Grose seldom drops the matter of social propriety in general and Quint's social improprieties in particular. Again questioned about Miles and Quint, Mrs. Grose reveals that there had been occasions "When they had been about together quite as if Quint were his tutor—and a very grand one—and Miss Jessel only for the little lady." So there we have it. Quint did *not* know his place. A gentleman *he*? Never! Yet here we find him, not belowstairs with Mrs. Grose, where maybe he belongs, but kiting about like a gentleman-tutor, and a very grand one at that, with the young gentleman in tow. Why, that —that—valet! We can almost see Mrs. Grose bridle and hear her sniff.

She did venture "to criticise the propriety, to hint at the incongruity, of so close an alliance, and even to go so far on the subject as a frank overture to Miss Jessel would take her. Miss Jessel had, with a very high manner about it, requested her to mind her business." Poor Mrs. Grose, surrounded by the governess' high and the valet's grand manner —neither easy to bear, though at least Miss Jessel, being a lady and a governess, was entitled to make her weight felt, while Quint—

Rebuked by Miss Jessel, Mrs. Grose next "directly approached little Miles. What she had said to him, since I pressed, was that *she* liked to see young gentlemen not forget their station." That note again. How can anyone doubt the housekeeper's sensitivity to intercaste propriety (or impropriety), to the socially congruous (or incongruous), to one's station (or forgetting one's station)? The point is worth dwelling on because her sensitivity was at the root of her manifestly seething hatred of Peter Quint. With this in mind, examine the dialogue of two more inquisitions that the governess conducts, Mrs. Grose being the examinee, not overlooking the use of words like "difference," "rank," "condition," "lady," and "dreadfully below." When the governess asks why Mrs. Grose did not report Quint's doings to the master:

Mrs. Grose. I dare say I was wrong. But really I was afraid.
The Governess. Afraid of what?
Mrs. Grose. Of things that man could do. Quint was so clever—he was so deep.
The Governess. You weren't afraid of anything else? Not of his effect—?
Mrs. Grose. His effect?
The Governess. On innocent little precious lives. They were in your charge.
Mrs. Grose. No, they weren't in mine! The master believed in him and placed him here because he was supposed not to be quite in health and the country air so good for him. So he had everything to say. Yes . . . even about *them.*
The Governess. Them—that creature? And you could bear it!
Mrs. Grose. No. I couldn't—and I can't now!

Whereupon Mrs. Grose bursts into tears, such is her loathing of "that man" even in retrospect. But on to the next grilling:

The Governess. I must have it now. . . . Come, there was something between them.
Mrs. Grose. There was everything.
The Governess. In spite of the difference—?
Mrs. Grose. Oh of their rank, their condition. . . . *She* was a lady.
The Governess. Yes—she was a lady.
Mrs. Grose. And he so dreadfully below.
The Governess. The fellow was a hound.
Mrs. Grose (considering "as if it were perhaps a little a case for a sense of shades"). I've never seen one like him. He did what he wished.
The Governess. With *her*?
Mrs. Grose. With them all.
The Governess. It must have been also what *she* wished!
Mrs. Grose. Poor woman—she paid for it!
The Governess. Then you do know what she died of?
Mrs. Grose. No—I know nothing. I wanted not to know; I was glad enough I didn't; and I thanked heaven she was well out of this!
The Governess. Yet you had then your idea—
Mrs. Grose. Of her real reason for leaving? Oh yes—as to that. She couldn't have stayed. Fancy it here—for a governess! And afterwards I imagined —and I still imagine. And what I imagine is dreadful.
The Governess. Not so dreadful as what *I* do.

This dialogue presents the reader with the same old choice. He may fasten upon Mrs. Grose's grim, ex-post-facto imaginings and upon the governess' still more dreadful imaginings and supply concrete details of his own, beginning with "There was everything between" Miss Jessel and Quint, who "did what he liked" with the former governess—in fact, "with them all." Though the governess declares him a hound, one wonders whether she does not envisage him rather as another animal, an imperious stallion lording it over *all* the inmates of the stable, including the foals. But each theorizer should be left to his own imaginings, as James intended that he should be.

The nonapparitionist had rather explore other possibilities of the dialogue. Mrs. Grose's mind seems to be focused, as usual, upon the matter of caste. Alas, that Quint had been left "in charge," as she has made abundantly clear earlier, had been much too free (in exercising his authority?), had had everything to say (about how the household should be run?), and had done what he wished (in ordering about everybody at Bly, including Miss Jessel?). All this despite the appalling difference in the ranks and conditions of Quint and Miss Jessel. *She* was a lady, while he, only a valet, a servant, was so dreadfully below. Even so, Mrs. Grose does not directly confirm the governess' summing up, "The fellow was a hound," apparently considering this "a little a case for a sense of shades." Nor does she verbally validate the governess' statement, "It must have been also what *she* wished," though according to the governess Mrs. Grose's "face signified that it had been indeed." How much credence can be paid the governess' interpretations of Mrs. Grose's facial expressions is debatable. Fancy such a state of affairs for a governess at Bly, lacking (though a lady) the authority of the present governess, subject to the dreadfully inferior Quint. She couldn't have stayed: thank heaven she got well out of the predicament.

We can never be sure what Miss Jessel's actual reaction to her life at Bly may have been. From Mrs. Grose's earlier testimony we know only that the former governess left Bly "at the end of the year, to go home, as she said, for a short holiday, to which the time she had put in had certainly given her a right." We know also that Mrs. Grose was expecting her back at the very moment the report of her death reached Bly. The implication is obviously that she liked her job well enough to return to it after a short, well-earned holiday. If so, what are we now to make of Mrs. Grose's "idea" of Miss Jessel's "real reason for leaving," namely, "She couldn't have stayed. Fancy it here—for a governess"? If she was, thank heaven, "well out of this," and shared Mrs. Grose's suffering over the allegedly warped chain of command at Bly, how mystifying to be expecting her momentarily to rejoin the agonizing, subjugated household.

Two more bits of interchange remain to perplex the reader. Note James's artful use of the indefinite "something," "everything," and "it" in the following:

The Governess. Come, there was something between them.
Mrs. Grose. There was everything.

Mrs. Grose. He did what he wished. . . . With them all.
The Governess. It must have been also what *she* wished!
Mrs. Grose. Poor woman—she paid for it!!

We need not expatiate on how the governess would gloss the mysterious words. Let us recall, instead, the expression "There was bad blood between them." Could there have been differences of opinion, quarrels, bad blood between the valet and the governess? Or does Mrs. Grose simply mean that between them there was a vast distance socially, uncounted degrees in the social scale? Did Miss Jessel comply with the master's arrangement putting Quint in charge and find his regime less heinous than Mrs. Grose did? Did she then pay for her compliance with his orders when Quint became still more free in wielding his authority? Or did she pay for opposing him, suffering his vindictiveness? Deponent saith not. None of the possibilities can be ruled out.

At one time James had in mind "the social hierarchy in this country—the grades and shelves and stages of relative gentility . . . in which each stage . . . has something or someone below them . . . on whom, the snubbed and despised from above, may wreak resentment by doing, below, as they are done by." The "succession or ladder of examples" in *The Turn of the Screw* is not obviously or patly delineated, but it does cast its shadow athwart many a character, many a motivation in the tale.

Upon the top rung stands the master, the bachelor of Harley Street, of gentle birth and rich besides. After employing the governess he pays absolutely no mind to her or to her "slighted charms." But she is still a lady, God save the mark, and in supreme authority. She allows Mrs. Grose to forget neither fact. The late Miss Jessel was also a lady who once had occasion in a very high manner to request the housekeeper to mind her own business. Poor Mrs. Grose, reeling upon her rung, battered by haughty pressure from aloft. Not to mention the pressures exerted by *that man, that creature* who in Mrs. Grose's never concealed opinion had clambered from whatever lowly rung was properly his to one much higher, where he assumed the airs of a very grand tutor and stood haughtily dispensing orders to his betters, to everyone!

One wonders whether Mrs. Grose worked off her resentment below in accordance with the treatment she has received from above. Perhaps it is just as well that James did not take time to define her treatment of old Luke and the various maids. His recital might have made Cinderella's fate at the hands of her stepmother and stepsisters seem pallid.

XV. *As a Woman Reads Another*

At the end of Chapter XII the governess writes of Mrs. Grose, "as a woman reads another—she could see what I myself saw." The remark, as a commentary on their relationship in general, contains about equal portions of truth and falsity. It is true that Mrs. Grose shows perspicacity about the governess' character and motives in, say, Chapter A, false because in Chapter B Mrs. Grose is dumbfounded by some action of the governess, or by her words, which frequently leave the housekeeper at a loss.

There is a considerable irony in the governess' saying of Mrs. Grose "as a woman *reads* another," for Mrs. Grose apparently cannot read and write at all. When the governess hands her the letter from Miles's headmaster, she puts her hands behind her, shakes her head sadly, and says, "Such things are not for me, Miss." Though this demurrer *could* mean that dealing with the child's educational problems is no affair of hers, being rather the governess' province, for once the governess is probably right, as other evidence of Mrs. Grose's illiteracy is plentiful. When she threatens to write the uncle, the governess tactlessly inquires,

" 'Do you mean you'll write—?' Remembering she couldn't, I caught myself up. 'How do you communicate?' " Mrs. Grose replies, " 'I tell the bailiff. *He* writes'."

Her grammar is what one might expect of the unlettered. "And him who thinks so well of you"; "you never see nothing, my sweet"; "he do hate worry"—and on and on. The homely solecisms pour out, to some of us a refreshment, really, after a glut of the governess' elegant but mannered, sometimes unbearably prim talk. ("An unknown man in a lonely place is a permitted object of fear to a young woman privately bred.") Critics who call attention to the name Grose and its symbolic force have in mind primarily her grammatical failings, though if apparitionists they may also agree with the governess' judgment that Mrs. Grose is "a magnificent monument to the blessing of a want of imagination," unable to share the governess' refined intuitions, perceptions—and visions.

Like her grammar, Mrs. Grose's vocabulary leaves a good deal to be desired. Her active fund of words is not broad in scope. Yet her verbal limitations are seldom recognized by the governess. Once, to be sure, when the governess asks, "You like them with the spirit to be naughty? . . . So do I! . . . But not to the degree to contaminate—" and Mrs. Grose blankly echoes the big word, the governess realizes that "my big word left her at a loss." For the most part, however, the self-centered governess, with her own remarkable vocabulary, races on, hysterically proffering inductions, analyses, diagnoses, and alarming hypotheses to an uncomprehending auditor.

Sometimes the two suffer a nearly complete breakdown in communications of which the governess remains blithely unaware. Were she as sensitive to the intellectual gap between them as she is to the social chasm, she might realize how repeatedly they talk at cross purposes. Several scenes indicate that the governess might as well be speaking Parsee, for all of Mrs. Grose. If Mrs. Grose's reaction to "contaminate" is typical, then she betrays her lack of comprehension of a word by a kind of puzzled repetition of it. Here are other samples—two out of a dozen or more that could be quoted.

The Governess. [The female apparition] only fixed the child.
Mrs. Grose. Fixed her? . . .
The Governess. With a determination—indescribable. With a kind of fury of intention.
Mrs. Grose. Intention?

The example that should be everybody's favorite comes from an interchange at the end of Chapter VIII. Only the governess' Parsee need be quoted; she does most of the talking anyhow, while a probably stupefied Mrs. Grose stands by with her mouth agape. "You reminded him that Quint was only a base menial? . . . He then prevaricated about it—he said he hadn't? . . . Did he put that to you as a justification? . . . If Quint—on your remonstrance at the time you speak of—was a base menial, one of the things Miles said to you . . . was that you were another." If Mrs. Grose did not command our respect despite her ignorance and if the governess were not here treating an extremely serious matter, the effect of the passage would be as richly comic as Feste's confounding Sir Andrew with "Pigrogromitus, of the Vapians passing the equinoctial of Quebus" and "I did impeticos thy gratillity."

Apparitionists who urge the significance of Mrs. Grose's "validations" of the governess' conclusions about the wickedness of the live Quint and Miss Jessel should bear in mind the paucity of big words in the housekeeper's vocabulary. In Chapter VII the governess tries describing what she has seen in Seizure 3 (Miss Jessel at the lake the first time): "[The figure was] handsome—very, very . . . wonderfully handsome. But infamous." And Mrs. Grose, slowly approaching the speaker, says, "Miss Jessel—*was* infamous. . . . They were both infamous." The dash may signify, eloquently, the pause before she made her stab at the unfamiliar word. What is the likelihood that "infamous" would be in the vocabulary of the dear old illiterate whom "contaminate," "effect," "fixed," and "intention" perplex? As for "base menial," "prevaricated," "remonstrance," and "justification," Mrs. Grose probably exclaimed "Laws!" (mentally, at least) after each one of them.

The use of "justification" here, incidentally, should put the reader on his guard when another form of the word occurs at a crucial stage after Seizure 7, when the estrangement between Flora and the governess is complete, the child having spent the night in Mrs. Grose's quarters. Under pressure (as usual), Mrs. Grose admits that Flora has told her, in shocking language, some really horrible things about the governess. The latter, seizing this news as proof that Flora is now completely under the sway of her evil adversary, Miss Jessel, cries "Oh, thank God! . . . It so justifies me!" And Mrs. Grose replies, "It does that, Miss!" A careful study of this "verification" within its context will show that the meaning of the word, again, eludes Mrs. Grose. For all she knows, "justifies" could mean "indict," or "prove guilty."

The governess would be more sensitive to these occasions when she leaves her companion linguistically behind if she weren't hopelessly absorbed in the fevered workings of her own mind and also if she gave Mrs. Grose more of a chance to speak uninterrupted. Study any of the tense dialogues, especially those in which Torquemada is trying to ferret out information, and notice how the dashes in Mrs. Grose's speeches proliferate. These show the sentences she has not been allowed to finish. The governess usually obliges by finishing them for her—in a fashion which may or may not represent Mrs. Grose's real intent but which supplies additional grist to the governess' busy mill.

The effect of at least one such interruption is irresistibly comic to nonapparitionist eyes. To Mrs. Grose's relief, when the governess agrees firmly to drop the cruel charge against Miles which she has trumped up from the headmaster's letter, Mrs. Grose wipes her mouth twice and begins, "Would you mind, Miss, if I used the freedom—" Since the governess, as is her wont, seizes the conversational ball and rushes off with it, finishing Mrs. Grose's question for her, one can only guess at what Mrs. Grose had in mind. "Would you mind, Miss, if I used the freedom—to give you a bit of advice? Then try to get more sleep and think less of the master" is a plausible way to end the utterance. But the governess, misled by the mouth-wiping, produces a different ending—doubtless to Mrs. Grose's stupefaction: "To kiss me? No!" Whereupon the governess enfolds Mrs. Grose "in my arms and after we had embraced like sisters felt still more fortified."

One of the rich ironies of the tale is that in spite of the formidable semantic, temperamental, and social barriers between the two women the governess is persuaded of their accord. Like the women's magazine, she would light on togetherness as the essential ingredient of their relationship. Note the evidence of this conviction, widely scattered through the novel from Chapter VI through Chapter XXI: "It took . . . more than that particular passage to place us together"; "What was settled between us accordingly that night was that we thought we might bear things together"; "So for a little we faced it once more together"; "I couldn't have borne the strain alone"; "Yes, it was a joy, and we were still shoulder to shoulder."

The governess is too sanguine in some of these joyful asseverations of unity, for she and Mrs. Grose (to mix a metaphor) often stand shoulder to shoulder only to lock horns. In this connection, readers who are far removed in time and space from the setting of *The Turn of the Screw* will find illuminating the attitude of a writer who grew up in a milieu not vastly different from Bly. In *Left Hand, Right Hand!* Sir Osbert Sitwell has a great deal to say about Davis, the Sitwell children's nurse at Renishaw, whose station was approximately the same as Mrs. Grose's and who, like the housekeeper, had formerly been servant to the children's grandmother. Sir Osbert remarks that with their governess Davis carried on the usual nurse-versus-governess feud, "a feud that perhaps has its origin in the same sort of state of tension that exists between man and monkey, where each sees in the other a slight resemblance to itself."

One scene in Chapter VI may give off a reflection of this kind of traditional strife. The governess compels Mrs. Grose to resurrect her memories of the trying days at Bly when Quint "had everything to say . . . even about *them*"—the children. "Them—that creature?" the governess cries. "And you could bear it?" Mrs. Grose replies, "No. I couldn't—and I can't now," and demonstrates how the thought galls her by bursting into tears. What exactly does she mean by "and I can't now"? That she cannot endure, even in retrospect, Quint's being in charge? Or does she mean that even now she cannot bear seeing another —namely, the governess—exercise supreme authority over her beloved children?

Not that the single word "feud," any more than "togetherness," adequately describes the complex relationship between the women. Still, the reader would be ill-advised to overlook the evidence already presented that Mrs. Grose has her moments of incredulity, of doubts about the governess' sanity, even of defiance. The homely "Laws" and "Lord," often on the housekeeper's lips, usually signal these reactions. When the governess insists that at a certain moment Flora is with Miss Jessel while Miles is with Quint, what is Mrs. Grose's spontaneous reaction? "Lord, Miss!" When Mrs. Grose sanely asks the governess to explain the motives of Quint and Miss Jessel in haunting the children, the governess says the blackguards return to ply Miles and Flora with the evil which while living they were able to instill in their victims, "to keep up the work of demons." At this monstrous "explanation" Mrs. Grose exclaims under her breath, "Laws!"

Most readers recognize in the oath the same old expression of incredulity, but the governess, habitually obsessed with her own catapulting train of thought, construes "Laws" as Mrs. Grose's "real acceptance of my further proof of what in the bad time [while the demons were still alive] . . . must have occurred." It is hard to say which is the grosser misrepresentation, "acceptance" or "further proof." The governess goes on to construe Mrs. Grose's exclamation as "the plain assent of her experience to whatever depth of depravity I found credible in our brace of scoundrels." Such are the perils of talking at cross purposes. Who could have predicted that so modest a little monosyllable as "Laws," uttered under the breath, would add fuel to the already raging fire?

Mutual misconstructions, then, not to say occasionally total lack of comprehension, beset both women, so that the governess may grasp the significance of "Laws" no more fully than Mrs. Grose is able to cope with "base menials." But this does not mean that floundering in the linguistic morass so cripples Mrs. Grose's judgment that she cannot grasp a few truths about their predicament. At the outset in this section we admitted that the governess is partially accurate in stating that Mrs. Grose can divine certain things about her "as a woman reads another." What we had in mind, specifically, was Mrs. Grose's obvious comprehension of the font of the governess' troubles—unrequited love for the master.

The governess gives her the clue early in the story, in Chapter I, during a pregnant little exchange about Flora and Miles:

Mrs. Grose. If you think well of this one!—
The Governess. Yes! if I do—?
Mrs. Grose. You *will* by carried away by the little gentleman!
The Governess. Well, that, I think, is what I came for—to be carried away. I'm afraid, however . . . I'm rather easily carried away. I was carried away in London!
Mrs. Grose. In Harley Street?
The Governess. In Harley Street.
Mrs. Grose. Well, Miss, you're not the first—and you won't be the last.
The Governess. Oh I've no pretensions . . . to being the only one.

Yet to be the only one is precisely the hope to which the governess clings, and Mrs. Grose shows, in various ways, a consistent recognition of that hope. As late as Chapter XXI, after Flora openly turns against the governess, the latter says, "Flora has now her grievance, and she'll work it to the end." Mrs. Grose asks, "Yes, Miss; but to *what* end?" The governess replies, "Why that of dealing with me to her uncle. She'll make me out to him the lowest creature—!" It is Mrs. Grose's turn to interrupt, and there is a world of perspicacity in her exclamation: "And him who thinks so well of you!" Even the governess shows, in her own fashion, her acceptance of the relevance of this remark by adding, "He has an odd way—it comes over me now— . . . of proving it!"

XVI. *The Best of the Burden?*

IN CHAPTER VI the governess writes of Mrs. Grose, "I was not even sure that in spite of her exemption [from seeing Quint] it was she who had the best of the burden." The reader is not sure either and wonders intermittently why Mrs. Grose puts up with all she is called on to endure instead of seeking extrication. Why doesn't she ask the bailiff to write the master long before she knows deliverance is in sight? She doesn't for a variety of reasons, apart from those suggested above, namely, that she recognizes the governess' social and intellectual superiority and respects her office. Ignorance usually breeds superstition: maybe to begin with she is inclined to believe in ghosts in general, hence in the ghosts at Bly in particular—until the evidence of her own eyes convinces her that there are no such things.

Not to be forgotten also is the persuasiveness the governess exercises upon her. The governess' magnificent eloquence has taken in others to whom the adjectives ignorant, gullible, uneducated, and unsophisticated ordinarily never apply, involving them so completely in her point of view that she has them converted irrevocably to the proposition that evil spirits haunt the story. If the housekeeper were to surrender unconditionally to the governess' grim hypothesis, she would be in good company.

Then there is her placid temperament, so subtly defined by James as a contrast to the governess' volatility. The best descriptions of this side of the "stout simple plain clean wholesome woman" are the governess':

I could feel her, when she surveyed them [the children] with her large white arms folded and the habit of serenity in all her look, thank the Lord's mercy that if they were ruined the pieces would still serve. Flights of fancy gave place, in her mind, to a steady fireside glow. . . . Mrs. Grose watched them with positive placidity.

I secured five minutes with her in the housekeeper's room, where, in the twilight, amid a smell of lately-baked bread, but with the place all swept and garnished, I found her sitting in pained placidity before the fire. So I see her still, so I see her best: facing the flame from her straight chair in the dusky shining room, a large clean picture of the "put away"—of drawers closed and locked and rest without a remedy.

This is not a woman given to impulsive action even though her placidity be pained, her natural serenity ruffled. Where the governess gives way to flights of fancy—and to hysteria—Mrs. Grose radiates a steady fireside glow and apparently forgets her troubles by going off to bake a loaf of bread. She has the happy faculty of seeing "in our little charges nothing but their beauty and amiability, their happiness and cleverness," which nonapparitionists believe are all there is to see. When the governess harshly tries to shatter the picture, Mrs. Grose is apt to retreat with an air of resignation, or, as the governess puts it, into "her patience under my pain."

Another very lovable thing about Mrs. Grose is her reluctance to tattle—on the governess or anybody else. When the governess subjects her to one of the earliest questionings about Miss Jessel, the housekeeper surrenders only two answers before saying, "Well, Miss—she's gone. I won't tell tales." Even the governess recognizes the virtue (though it doesn't deter her from her inquisitions) and says, "I appreciate . . . the great decency of your not having hitherto spoken; but the time has certainly come to give me the whole thing." In addition to her scruples against tale-bearing and her consequent "decency" in such matters, she has other less noble, but good and sufficient, reasons for holding her tongue. She has suffered in the past for not keeping her own counsel. Her complaint to Miss Jessel about the impropriety of Quint's behavior has provoked from the former governess the request that she mind her business.

Then why not pour out the whole lamentable story of Quint's usurpation of powers not rightfully his—and also the story of the present governess' weird behavior, for that matter—to the ultimate authority, the master in Harley Street? Because—"Well, he didn't like tale-bearing—he hated complaints. He was terribly short with anything of that kind." Even when desperate enough to urge the governess to summon him, Mrs. Grose takes thought: "Yes, he do hate worry." Finally, when the jig is up for the governess, who has thoroughly terrified and estranged Flora, her exposure to the uncle is inevitable, and she insists that Mrs. Grose take Flora away from Bly straight to her uncle, the kind woman's first thought is "Only to tell on you—?"

At the end of Chapter XXIV, with Flora in a delirium and Miles dead, how bitterly Mrs. Grose must regret not having "told on" the governess, no matter what the price to be paid in incurring the master's grave displeasure. But suffering regret is apparently not a new experience for the poor soul. After Seizure 6 the governess tries to fasten the blame for all the agony at Bly on the employer for leaving the children with Quint and Miss Jessel. Mrs. Grose turns pale and insists, in a vociferous *mea culpa*, that he "didn't really in the least know them. The fault's mine." The fault for what? For not "telling on" Quint or Miss Jessel? For allowing the governess to believe them to be monsters? Or does the blood drain from her face with the shock of realizing she is about to repeat the mistake of not tattling in time? Perhaps so, because almost in the next breath she informs the governess with remarkable force that she needn't bother to tell the uncle anything: "*I'll* tell him."

There are other signs that Mrs. Grose, for all her lack of book-learning, is able to profit from errors committed in the past. After Seizures 1 and 2 her "identification" of the figure on the tower and the face at the window as the late Peter Quint has served as a kind of catalytic agent to the seething cauldron at Bly, leaving her "a receptacle of lurid things" with no choice but to offer "her mind to my disclosures as, had I wished to mix a witch's broth and proposed it with assurance, she would have held out a large clean saucepan." What course is she to take, then, after Seizure 3, when the governess announces that Miss Jessel has appeared to her and Flora at the lake? Is she going to oblige again by identifying the apparition as the late governess?

To arrive at an answer, one might begin with a review of what is known about Miss Jessel. Watch for clues to Mrs. Grose's attitude toward her. To the governess, who passes on the information to Douglas, the uncle has characterized her as "a young lady whom they had had the misfortune to lose. She had done for them quite beautifully—she was a most respectable person—till her death." A question by one of Douglas's auditors reinforces this "character reference": "And what did the former governess die of?—of so much respectability?"

This testimony does not of course satisfy the governess, who insistently questions Mrs. Grose about her predecessor at her earliest opportunity:

The Governess. What was the lady who was here before?
Mrs. Grose. The last governess? She was also young and pretty—almost as young and almost as pretty, Miss, even as you. . . .
The Governess. Did *she* see anything in the boy—?
Mrs. Grose. That wasn't right? She never told me.
The Governess. Was she careful—particular?
Mrs. Grose. About some things—yes.
The Governess. But not about all?
Mrs. Grose. Well . . . I won't tell tales. . . .
The Governess. Did she die here?
Mrs. Grose. No—she went off.

From this incomplete, not altogether willingly given account, the charitable reader gains one impression of Miss Jessel, the uncharitable quite another. She was pretty and young. If she saw anything in Miles that "wasn't right," she kept it to herself. She was careful, particular,

about, say, the children's studies, dress, and manners, though she and
Mrs. Grose did not perhaps agree about their diet. If so, Mrs. Grose,
no tattletale, is unwilling to specify what their differences were. At the
year's end "our young lady" (a phrase that sounds both respectful and
affectionate) went home for a deserved vacation. Pressed for details
about her death which are unknown to her, Mrs. Grose firmly puts an
end to the interrogation, unwilling to gossip further about "our young
lady," now dead.

For that uncharitable interpretress the present governess, however, it
is an easy step from Mrs. Grose's comments about Miss Jessel's youth
and beauty, about her death from causes unknown to Mrs. Grose, and
about her carefulness in *some* things but not, by implication, in all, to
the ghost of Miss Jessel: "a figure of . . . unmistakeable horror and
evil," "a horror of horrors," a "pale and ravenous demon," "my vile
predecessor . . . Dishonoured and tragic . . . in her black dress, her hag-
gard beauty and her unutterable woe."

But see how the linking of the late Miss Jessel with Seizure 3 strikes
Mrs. Grose. Here is the governess' report at the beginning of Chapter
VII:

The Governess. Flora *saw*!
Mrs. Grose. She has told you?
The Governess. Not a word. . . .
Mrs. Grose. Then how do you know?
The Governess. I was there—I saw with my eyes: saw she was perfectly
aware.
Mrs. Grose. Do you mean aware of *him*?
The Governess. No—of *her*. Another person—this time; but a figure of
quite as unmistakeable horror and evil: a woman in black, pale and dread-
ful—with such an air also, and such a face! . . .
Mrs. Grose. Was she someone you've never seen?
The Governess. Never. But someone the child has. Someone *you* have. My
predecessor—the one who died.
Mrs. Grose. Miss Jessel?
The Governess. Miss Jessel. You don't believe me?
Mrs. Grose. How can you be sure?

The Governess. Then ask Flora—*she's* sure! No, for God's sake *don't*! She'll say she isn't—she'll lie! . . . Flora doesn't want me to know.
Mrs. Grose. It's only then to spare you. . . .
The Governess. Oh we must clutch at *that*—we must cling to it! . . . For the woman's a horror of horrors.
Mrs. Grose. Tell me how you know.
The Governess. Then you admit it's what she was?
Mrs. Grose. Tell me how you know.

Notable in this dialogue are Mrs. Grose's sensible questions opposed to the wild irrationality of the governess' lines, replete, as they so often are, with the *non-sequitur*, the improvisatory, the hysterical. James could hardly have made more conspicuous Mrs. Grose's unwillingness to follow the path the governess is trying to push her down. The governess begins the scene by throwing herself into Mrs. Grose's arms and feeling "her incredulity" as she lies there. "You don't believe me?" the governess presses Mrs. Grose in the face of the latter's apparently persistent refusal to accept her insane assertions. Consider also the effect of Mrs. Grose's repeated efforts to pin the governess down to the facts: "Then how do you know? . . . How can you be sure? . . . Tell me how you know. . . . Tell me how you know."

Mrs. Grose has been a party to "identifying" Quint, but she is not going to fall into that trap again. Instead, she tries to reduce the governess to relevancy by repeating the only concrete detail which the governess has so far advanced in her description of the new horror.

Mrs. Grose. The person was in black, you say?
The Governess. In mourning—rather poor, almost shabby. But—yes—with extraordinary beauty.

Mrs. Grose steadfastly declines to find the extraordinary beauty and shabby mourning as meaningful as she has previously found the lack of gentility, the borrowed clothes, the handsomeness, and the hatlessness in the governess' report of the earlier seizures. Compare a later scene after the governess has accused the children of consorting secretly with the ghosts of Quint and the figure whom she has identified, to her own satisfaction, as Miss Jessel's:

The Governess. They're not mine—they're not ours. They're his and they're hers!

Mrs. Grose. Quint's and that woman's?

Take into account that Mrs. Grose again refuses to identify "that woman" as Miss Jessel, whom she elsewhere scrupulously calls "a lady."

Her unwavering refusal from first to last makes a mockery of the governess' claim, "I found . . . I had only to ask her how, if I had 'made it up,' I came to be able to give, of each of the persons appearing to me, a picture disclosing, to the last detail, their special marks—a portrait on the exhibition of which she had instantly recognized and named them." The truth is of course that the vague details about the second apparition do *not* spell Miss Jessel to the housekeeper—either instantly or ever— and certainly she scrupulously avoids connecting the name of her late colleague with the beautiful, black-clad horror that is a figment of the governess' sick brain.

Mrs. Grose remains steadfast about one other matter—the goodness and innocence of the children. Try as the governess will, she cannot shake Mrs. Grose's stand. From the prologue, which tells that the housekeeper has formerly superintended Flora, of whom she was extremely fond, until the very end of the novel, when Flora has moved bag and baggage out of the governess' bedroom and into Mrs. Grose's quarters, the good woman never deviates from her devotion. When the governess seems on the point of interrogating Miles about the late Quint, "Ah don't try him" breaks from Mrs. Grose. As for the boy's friendship with the valet, Mrs. Grose emphatically declares, "Oh it wasn't *him*" who was responsible for striking it up, but Quint. Nor is she willing for Flora to be linked with Quint, for "the little lady doesn't remember. She never heard or knew."

The governess' charge that Flora has been communing with Miss Jessel's ghost but will lie about the communion if challenged elicits from Mrs. Grose the immediate protest, "Ah how *can* you," and she inquires staunchly, "Isn't it just a proof of her blessed innocence?" As the governess speculates evilly about what Quint and Miss Jessel "must . . .

have succeeded in making" of Miles, his defender promptly interjects, "Ah nothing that's not nice *now*! . . . And if he was so bad then as that comes to, how is he such an angel now?" Resigned at last to having everything out before the tribunal in Harley Street, the governess assures Mrs. Grose, "Well, you shan't suffer," to which the children's champion retorts, "The children shan't!"

At the end of the strenuous hike around the lake to find Flora, Mrs. Grose throws herself on her knees and clasps in a long embrace the child they have just recovered. The governess envies Mrs. Grose, as well she might, "the simplicity of *her* relation" with the little girl. A moment later, as the spasm of Seizure 7 grips her and she hurls her fantastic charges in Flora's face, she becomes "aware of having Mrs. Grose also, and very formidably, to reckon with." Instantly, the housekeeper and her beloved child stand—where they have always stood and where they belong—"united," but this time "united, as it were, in shocked opposition to me."

XVII. *Mrs. Grose's Motherly Breast*

MRS. GROSE does not reserve for the children alone her protective instincts, her readiness to defend those she cares for, her loyalty, and her love. She has sufficiently large store to accord the governess herself a generous portion of all these at a time when, Heaven knows, the poor girl desperately needs them. The housekeeper's deep affection for the young lady from Hampshire lends a complication, an added dimension—and a poignancy—to *The Turn of the Screw* to which nobody has paid any attention.

What could be better calculated to stir the maternal instincts than the arrival of a country girl conspicuously inexperienced and nervous and touchingly young? At twenty she is really, according to the law of many a land, only a child herself, and the note of affection for her creeps into Mrs. Grose's speeches at a very early stage of the game. To the girl's first query about her predecessor, Mrs. Grose replies, as we have seen, "The last governess? She was also young and pretty—almost as young and almost as pretty, Miss, even as you." When the young, pretty miss begins to share her considerable, highly vocal sufferings with her new friend, Mrs. Grose's feelings for her become broader and deeper, comprising solicitude and compassion as well as affection. The concisest method of exhibiting this complex of feelings is to quote in chronological order a generous sampling of passages in which they are exposed.

> After Seizure 2 the governess and Mrs. Grose have to live as best they can with "my dreadful liability to impressions of the order so vividly exemplified, and my companion's knowledge henceforth—a knowledge half consternation and half compassion—of that liability. . . . She herself had seen nothing, not the shadow of a shadow, and nobody in the house but the governess was in the governess' plight; yet she . . . ended by showing me . . . an awestricken tenderness, a deference to my more than questionable privilege, of which the very breath has remained with me as that of the sweetest of human charities."

> I must have shown her . . . a front of miserable defeat. It brought out again all her compassion for me, and at the renewed touch of her kindness my power to resist broke down. I burst . . . into tears; she took me to her motherly breast.

> I had already begun to perceive how, with the development of the conviction that . . . our young things could, after all, look out for themselves, she addressed her greatest solicitude to the sad case presented by their deputy-guardian.

> After Mrs. Grose's threat to have the bailiff write their employer, the governess asks, "And should you like him to write our story?" Mrs. Grose's eyes fill with tears as she kindly allows the governess the more dignified course of surrendering her hopes of martyrdom in her own way: "Ah Miss, *you* write!"

To be torn between affection, kindly solicitude, tenderness, and compassion for the agonizing twenty-year-old, on the one hand, and love for the children, eight and ten years of age, on the other, is not an easy fate. It is a pity the governess forces Mrs. Grose to choose between them because the housekeeper is eager to preserve the equilibrium. She is willing to perch atop the powder keg only under certain conditions, however. The main one, stated generally, is that her beloved young lady should do nothing to inflict pain on the even more beloved Flora and Miles.

Though several of the compacts that Mrs. Grose and the governess strike have already been alluded to, it would be convenient to examine them all together. There is no need for them, of course, until after the governess confides in Mrs. Grose her "dreadful liability to impressions of the order so vividly exemplified"—her liability to seizures. Then the need becomes suddenly grave, and the seemingly endless conferences follow thick, fast, and urgent. The proud governess never writes anything so undignified as an explicit revelation of the conditions Mrs. Grose lays down. She surrenders these conditions only obliquely. Still, it is not impossible to divine certain terms, despite the governess' continual artful casualness and indirection. Here is one of the key passages after Mrs. Grose surprises her glaring in the window:

There had been . . . a little service of tears and vows, of prayers and promises, a climax to the series of mutual challenges and pledges . . . on our retreating together . . . to have everything out. . . . What was settled between us . . . was that we thought we might bear things together . . . but it took me some time to be wholly sure of what my honest comrade was prepared for to keep terms with so stiff an agreement. . . . I could take the air in the court, at least, and there Mrs. Grose could join me.

The language in which the passage is couched suggests that of two attorneys dickering over points of law—with their promises, challenges, pledges, having everything out, settling, talk of keeping terms, and arriving at the stiff agreement. But the only specific clause that the governess bothers to mention is that she "can" (should it be "may"?) take the air in the court where the housekeeper can join her—i.e., keep an eye on her? As for other airy ramblings, unchaperoned and unobserved, elsewhere over the premises, or in any place save the court, are these now forbidden by the terms of the deal?

Other agreements which the governess volunteers to enter into, or upon which Mrs. Grose insists, are not so putative. Is the governess going to molest Miles about the headmaster's cryptic letter; is she going to say anything to the child about it? "Nothing at all," the governess

promises, whereupon Mrs. Grose says, "Then I'll stand by you. We'll
see it out." The governess, "giving her my hand to make it a vow,"
ardently echoes, "We'll see it out!" Despite her "shaking on it" to make
it a more or less formal kind of agreement, if not exactly a vow, the
governess goes back on her word before the story is done.

After the first episode with Miss Jessel, the governess is able to an-
nounce that she and Mrs. Grose are "of a common mind about the duty
of resistance to extravagant fancies" (i.e., fancifully positing the motives of the "ghosts," or possibly seeing them at all?) and about the
need "to keep our heads if we should keep nothing else." In this same
conference, in Chapter VIII, she assures Mrs. Grose that her main interest in the eerie subject of ghostly visitation has now "violently taken
the form of a search for the way to escape from it." Escape from it, indeed! She continues frantically to solicit supernatural attention as her
fancies burgeon ever more extravagantly and she loses her head morning, noon, and night—virtually all night, every night. Yet Chapter VIII
bristles with the governess' assurances and reassurances, and before its
end she is "able to asseverate to my friend that I was certain—which
was so much to the good—that *I* at least had not betrayed myself" during the seizure by the lake.

Three chapters later, after two more seizures, the governess draws "a
great security" from Mrs. Grose's "mere smooth aspect," especially
since both think it important not to arouse in the servants or the children "any suspicion of a secret flurry or of a discussion of mysteries."
Fortunately, in Mrs. Grose's "fresh face" there is nothing "to pass on to
others my horrible confidences." In exchange for this solace, or in
answer to an explicit, anxious inquiry from Mrs. Grose, the governess
can "engage that, to the world, my face should tell no tales." The housekeeper's smooth aspect shows that she is beginning to relax as time goes
on "without a public accident"—without, that is, the governess' "public" betrayal of her extravagant fancies to Miles and Flora.

Mrs. Grose's relaxation proves premature and unjustified. Even as
late as Chapter XI she has no way of knowing about the governess' failure to keep a single one of their bargains, about private as opposed to

public accidents, about what goes on elsewhere in the kindly old country mansion, in schoolroom and corridors and bedrooms when she is absent, about what transpires upstairs at night when she is belowstairs. The important point to bear in mind here is that she does her best, for the sake of the beloved children and the governess alike, to keep things on an even keel, to make life tolerable for all in the face of the most trying circumstances, to prevent an explosion. The pathetic little compacts she makes with the governess constitute part of her strategy.

This strategy, though ultimately ineffectual, is less haphazard than might be supposed, for, with experience, Mrs. Grose hits upon certain patterns in trying to deal with the sick girl. She seems now and again to grant the governess unqualified faith, even credence, partly because without the evidence of her own eyes, unavailable till late in the story, she does not in truth know *what* to believe, but chiefly because she must surrender to the inevitable. To follow any other course, such as too strong or direct questioning of the governess' reason, would be perilous.

Recall in this connection the drunken Cassio's insistence, "Why, very well, then, you must not think, then, that I am drunk," and the consequences when Montano blurts out, "Come, come, you're drunk." Mrs. Grose never dares be guilty of such bluntness. Instead, she must resignedly hold out the large clean saucepan to receive the witch's broth of the governess. In another, later, day a more educated Mrs. Grose might have served as a psychiatrist upon whose couch the frantic governess reposed, pouring out her witch's broth at twenty-five dollars an hour.

How dangerous would it be to contradict such a patient, or to question her sanity directly? The answer lies in the governess' "She believed me, I was sure, absolutely: if she hadn't I don't know what would have become of me, for I couldn't have borne the strain alone." This is scarcely the kind of desperation the governess is able or willing to conceal from her friend. The deluded governess, thinking she enjoys Mrs. Grose's total assent even after shockingly alienating Flora, fondly evaluates that assent, "if I might continue sure of that I should care but little what else happened. My support in the presence of disaster would be the same as it had been in my early need of confidence, and if my friend would answer for my honesty I would answer for all the rest."

Sometimes the governess seems to wring assent from her friend in much the same way the Russians are said to wring confessions from the accused, by a kind of prolonged, brain-numbing denial of rest. After Seizure 3 and a lengthy, gruelling inquisition in the afternoon, the governess again applies the screws in a second session late at night while the rest of the household slept until the exhausted housekeeper "went all the way with me as to its being beyond doubt that I had seen exactly what I had seen. . . . She wished, of course—a small blame to her!—to sink the whole subject" and, the governess might have added, to get some sleep.

Many further instances of the housekeeper's agreeing as a form of humoring could be marshalled, but one or two more will do. After Seizure 5 the governess erupts to really quite mad heights in her inductions concerning "our brace of scoundrels" and the demonic machinations that their ghosts now employ to possess the crafty, compliant children. Surely it is time to humor, and thus soothe, her again, and Mrs. Grose says sanely, "They *were* rascals! But what can they now do?"

In other words, "No matter what they may have been when alive, what can they do now that they are dead?" As for the placative "They *were* rascals" (with the emphasis on the tense) which Mrs. Grose throws out to the fulminating governess, avid for agreement and support, the governess and her apologists pounce on the sentence as still another objective confirmation of Miss Jessel's rascality, dead and alive. Under the spell of the governess' eloquent ravings, it is not easy to remember that, of the person whom the hard-pressed Mrs. Grose here calls a rascal, she has formerly said, "*She* was a lady"—"our young lady" who was "almost as young and almost as pretty, Miss, even as you."

For the benefit of apparitionists who require more evidence that humoring plays any part in the proceedings at Bly, a final example can be cited. After a taxing scene with Miles on the way to church in Chapter XIV, the governess admits "a pitiful surrender to agitation" and flees in panic back to the house. She consequently affords Mrs. Grose, Miles, and Flora, left behind at church, a unique opportunity to confer. Miles suggests that they say nothing of the governess' hysterical performance in the churchyard because she would "like it better." He adds, "We must do nothing but what she likes!"

He means, "Let's not n-o-t-i-c-e this latest outburst; we must humor her." How could the evidence of humoring be any clearer? Flora and Mrs. Grose sweetly agree to Miles's proposal. Their tactful silence, however, only renders the governess "freshly upset." In treating patients of this kind the nurses are, as the inelegant old saying has it, damned if they do and damned if they don't.

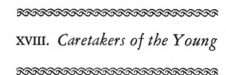

XVIII. *Caretakers of the Young*

WE HAVE suggested that Mrs. Grose doubts the governess' sanity. The housekeeper devotes "her greatest solicitude to the sad case presented" by the governess. "Sad case" implies an unfortunate patient, and Mrs. Grose in fact treats her exactly as if she were one, behaving at times like a forbearing, kindly nurse. The governess writes that Mrs. Grose accepts her weird version of "the truth," and does so "without directly impugning my sanity." The implication is that the housekeeper indirectly impugns it.

Indirection must of necessity be Mrs. Grose's way. Any other approach might prove dangerous since the governess is in charge at Bly and besides is intermittently violent. Tact (to say the least) therefore seems to be the dominant tone of what Mrs. Grose has to say on the subject of the young mistress's mental health. Echoes of her attitude filter through to the reader despite the fever of the governess' racing account. They would be amusing if the case were not, indeed, so sad.

Mrs. Grose exclaims, "Dear, dear —we must keep our heads!"—a tactful way of saying, "You must keep *your* head." When the two meet "once more in the wonder of it we were of a common mind about the duty of resistance to extravagant fancies. We were to keep our heads if we should keep nothing else." But the "extravagant fancies" apply solely to the governess; she is the sole participant in this dialogue who is in danger of losing her head.

There is a hint that Mrs. Grose occasionally abandons tact for frankness in "I found that . . . I had only to ask her how, if I had 'made it up,' I came to be able to give, of each of the persons appearing to me, a picture disclosing, to their last detail, their special marks." This means that after Seizure 3 Mrs. Grose throws out some such sentence as "I don't believe you've been seeing ghosts at all; I believe you've been making the whole thing up." It is a pity that the governess, generally so lavish in her quotations, does not see fit to record verbatim these expressions of her companion's skepticism so that the reader could study the exact words.

That Mrs. Grose's skepticism evolves slowly is doubtful. It seems rather to have been immediate, spontaneously following the governess' first confidence. When Mrs. Grose surprises her glaring in the window, the governess prefaces her revelations in Chapter V with "You came for me for church, of course, but I can't go," then tries in a piecemeal, disjointed fashion to give some account of the experience just suffered and of the one on the tower as well. A most interesting exchange ensues:

Mrs. Grose. Do you mean he's a stranger?
The Governess. Oh very much!
Mrs. Grose. Yet you didn't tell me?
The Governess. No—for reasons. But now that you've guessed—
Mrs. Grose. Ah I haven't guessed! How can I if *you* don't imagine?

Mrs. Grose's second question only underlines the abnormality of the governess' reactions to the first two seizures. Mrs. Grose's third question would be harder to gloss if the governess' response to it weren't so prompt and revealing. When Mrs. Grose says, "How can I if *you* don't imagine," the governess interprets the clause as an accusation: "I haven't guessed! How can I if *you* don't imagine"—i.e., "unless *you* are imagining [things]?" The governess' retort is immediate and vehement, "I don't in the very least." She is defending herself against the accusation; she is the girl with a guilty conscience and copious self-doubts who is later to write, significantly, of "my mere infernal imagination." Her interchange with Mrs. Grose also recalls the further accusation, attributable only to Mrs. Grose, that she has "made it up."

After protesting that she does not in the very least imagine things, she returns to the face at the window. "What *is* he? He's a horror. . . . He's—God help me if I know *what* he is!" The last exclamation, for all its hysterical intensity, is probably the governess' most honest revelation of her current state of mind. Indeed she does not know what the horror is. Like Mrs. Grose, however, she must have her suspicions, which she is not prepared to pursue so long as any alternative explanations can be invented or grasped at.

Confronted with her incoherence and inability to offer any really satisfactory alternative to the workings of an infernal imagination, Mrs. Grose does not allow her to proceed. Reverting to the governess' previous reference to church, she turns to the girl "with full inconsequence" and says abruptly, "It's time we should be at church." The assertion may be abrupt, but it is scarcely inconsequential. She wants to put an end to the fruitless, awkward, painful colloquy.

When the governess, in reply to her proposal, says, "Oh, I'm not fit for church," Mrs. Grose's marvelous rejoinder is "Won't it do you good?" The kind, wholesome woman has in mind the time-honored remedy for insanity—turning to God. King James recommended "fasting and prayer, and in-calling of the name of God." As Maria says of the "deranged" Malvolio, "Get him to say his prayers. Good Sir Toby, get him to pray." Or as the friends of another supposed lunatic urge in one of Barnaby Rich's short stories, "good neighbour forget these Idle speeches, which doeth so muche distemper you: and call upon God and he will surely helpe you."

In ministering to her "sad case," however, Mrs. Grose does not confine herself to such pious recommendations. As a nurse she does not give up easily, and she is on the whole very resourceful even though many condemn her for obtuseness. Once she tries what mid-twentieth-century readers recognize as shock treatment. The governess goes too far in her ranting when she assures Mrs. Grose that it "is only a question of time" till the spirits of Quint and Miss Jessel destroy the children, who will "perish in the attempt" to obey the ghostly summons. Mrs. Grose at once insists that their uncle must remove Miles and Flora from this danger and tries to induce the governess to invite him to come to the rescue. Since what the governess fears most is exposure to the man she passionately loves, she not only refuses but threatens to resign if Mrs. Grose herself appeals to him. Mrs. Grose's shock therapy nevertheless proves, temporarily, efficacious. After it the governess passes an entire month "without another encounter" with the demons.

In the middle of one of her endless interrogations of Mrs. Grose the governess records, "It was a straight question enough but levity was not our note." She never wrote a truer sentence, though she overlooks the fact that Mrs. Grose is not invariably so humorless as she on these dreary occasions. Not that the housekeeper is bubbling over with mirth either, yet one of her gambits, or nursing techniques, as it were, is to try to joke the governess out of an especially preposterous theory or attitude. In their conference about Miles's school, when the governess agrees that she too likes boys with spirit but not enough spirit to contaminate, to corrupt, their chums, Mrs. Grose asks, "Are you afraid he'll corrupt *you?*" The jest is not lost on the governess, unaccustomed though she is to being the cause that wit is in others. "She put the question with such a fine bold humor that with a laugh, a little silly doubtless, to match her own, I gave way for the time to the apprehension of ridicule."

Mrs. Grose has gained a momentary advantage through the use of the *reductio ad absurdum* (whether she knows the term or not), and not for the last time. When the governess insists that Flora communes with Miss Jessel, Mrs. Grose also reduces this insane proposition to the absurd: " '. . . after all, if she doesn't mind it—!' She even tried a grim joke. 'Perhaps she likes it!' " The joke almost works. The governess admits, "She brought me, for the instant, almost round." The phraseology here is worth a brief pause. Isn't "to bring someone round" an appropriate idiom to describe recalling a patient from some sort of fit?

Whether Mrs. Grose behaves more like a kindly nurse or a matron in a place of detention is another considerable question. Apart from the hint of the governess' being permitted to air herself only in the courtyard under Mrs. Grose's surveillance, two other intimations occur that the housekeeper is sometimes forced to behave like a warden or attendant in a sanatorium. They open up the grim prospect that the governess occasionally grows so violent as to require physical restraint. Lacking the proper equipment—strait jackets—what is Mrs. Grose to do? On the verge of Seizure 7, the one in which the governess gives herself away completely at the lake before Mrs. Grose's eyes, the governess peppers her manuscript with exclamation marks as she abandons herself to hysteria. Then she writes, "She always ended at these moments by getting possession of my hand, and in this manner she could at present still stay me."

The passage implies that Mrs. Grose habitually resorts to this drastic remedy—she "always ended, at these moments." The remedy seems effective, furthermore, as in the next paragraph the governess feels it necessary to add a phrase about "freeing" herself. Mrs. Grose may have a specific reason for trying to restrain the governess at this moment. Though inadequately clad for an excursion outdoors, the governess is bent on rushing to the lake in search of Flora, leaving Miles free, so she insists, to parley with the ghost of Quint upstairs in the schoolroom. Mrs. Grose, naturally unwilling to see her go or to accompany her, lags behind enroute, but by the time the governess reaches the water Mrs. Grose is close behind her. The governess believes that "whatever, to her apprehension, might befall me," Mrs. Grose has chosen "the exposure of sticking to me . . . as her least danger" compared to remaining in the house with Miles and Quint. Though no doubt ignorant of Ophelia's fate, could not the affectionately solicitous Mrs. Grose feel reluctant to allow the frenzied governess to charge unchaperoned to the water's edge?

Immediately after Seizure 3 the governess finds Mrs. Grose as soon as she can and hurls herself into her friend's arms. Is she inviting restraint? She feels Mrs. Grose's incredulity "as she held me. . . . Then as she released me I made it out to her." A bit later, Mrs. Grose "once more took my hand in both her own, holding it as tight as if to fortify me against the increase of alarm I might draw from this disclosure." "Fortify" indeed! The word has the aroma of the euphemism. Does it sometimes take two hands to restrain the patient? If so, Mrs. Grose is only reacting as one, alas, must to a case of complete, settled, and violent lunacy. The Elizabethans had a colorful way of putting all this. Page says, "Why, this passes, Master Ford! You are not to go loose any longer; you must be pinion'd." To cope with his raving, shrewish wife, one of Barnaby Rich's characters "gotte and pinioned her armes so faste, that she was not able to undoe them."

Significant changes in her keeper's treatment of the governess necessitate reverting to one of the understandings between them. Whether tacit or strictly defined, it is so important that Mrs. Grose's patient ministrations depend in a way upon the governess' keeping her part of this particular bargain. If worded like a commandment, it might read, "You shall not by facial expression, word, or deed betray to the children any trace of experiences with evil spirits, real or suppositious."

Why all this solemn concern shared by the governess and Mrs. Grose? Sir Osbert Sitwell, who was not quite Flora's age when *The Turn of the Screw* was published in 1898, affords a clue in *Left Hand, Right Hand!* In a section from Roger North's *The Lives of the Norths* (London, 1890) appended to Sir Osbert's volume, one reads that the children of the North family were carefully bred. "No inferior servants were permitted to entertain them, lest some . . . foolish notions and fables should steal into them." For that matter, Sir Osbert's father, Sir George, held strong convictions about the subject. He "would tell me," Sir Osbert records, "not to be frightened of the dark (he was very sympathetic about it) : there were no bogies in dark corners, no ogres or ghosts; they were only stupid and ignorant nurses' tales." Fortunately Sir George did not learn that Davis, the nurse of Edith and Osbert, was in the habit of telling them ghost stories though strictly forbidden to do so by their father.

Mrs. Grose and the governess, then, are reflecting the traditional point of view concerning ghost-free educational practices. In her manuscript the governess harps on few themes more consistently than this. The most revealing of quite a few expressions of how trapped she feels by the tradition follows:

I was confronted at last, as never yet, with all the risk attached even now to sounding my own horrid note [her theory concerning the evil spirits]. . . . I remember how I suddenly dropped . . . from the force of the idea that he [Miles] must know how he really, as they say, 'had' me. He could do what he liked . . . so long as I should continue to defer to the old tradition of the criminality of those caretakers of the young who minister to superstitions and fears. He 'had' me indeed, and in a cleft stick; for who would ever absolve me, who would consent that I should go unhung, if, by the faintest tremor of an overture, I were first to introduce into our perfect intercourse an element so dire?

What pain deferring to the old tradition obviously causes her! Without obtaining confessions that the children are doing what she believes them guilty of doing, how can she ever prove to the satisfaction of anybody, including herself, the existence of the unholy intercourse? Yet how can she set about extorting confessions without invading what she calls "Forbidden ground"? Ultimately the suffering this dilemma inflicts upon her—and it is greater than that which the mystery about Miles's school induces—overpowers her. She surrenders to "the strange impulse that I lately spoke of as my temptation." She embroils both Miles and Flora in her awful conjectures, and this means of course that she breaks her agreement with Mrs. Grose.

When does her kindly nurse first gain some awareness of her defection? In all probability after the governess flees precipitately from church leaving Mrs. Grose to escort the children home, to agree with them to ignore the governess' panicky behavior, and to discuss who knows what other hysterical performances about which the children possess knowledge. The governess is left "to study Mrs. Grose's odd face" as she returns with Miles and Flora, and must seek her out in her own quarters to "break down" her conspicuous silence. When she does so in the housekeeper's room, gone are Mrs. Grose's blandishments, the jokes, the humoring.

Instead, a note of rudeness if not outright defiance creeps into her attitude. When the governess explains that she returned from church to meet a friend (Miss Jessel in the schoolroom: Seizure 6), Mrs. Grose abruptly throws out, "A friend—you?" The high point in the interview, for the housekeeper, is the governess' declaration that she is now going to send for the uncle. "Oh Miss, in pity do," Mrs. Grose begs.

Marked though her change in attitude is in this scene, she remains uncertain about the objectivity of the ghosts. She must wait for the evidence of her own eyes. She has had all too many chances to observe the governess' postseizural behavior, but she has never been on hand when the governess believes herself to be actually in the presence of the revenants. Meantime, she finds waiting and uncertainty almost as cruel as does the governess. When the governess, on her way to the lake and Seizure 7 with Mrs. Grose in tow, promises "Beyond a doubt. You shall see [Flora and Miss Jessel together]," the abjectly grateful Mrs. Grose cries, "Oh thank you!"

Then she witnesses the shocking spectacle of the governess in the throes of a seizure in Flora's presence. She sees for herself that there is no such thing as the ghost of Miss Jessel. The cooperation, indulgence, submission, and alliance are at an end, though not the affection. The governess has forfeited the right to be nursed. Mrs. Grose's attitude henceforth is all firmness. Her principal concern must now be to get the child away from the maniac and keep her away. She must act at once. What a pity that it is already too late. Flora, literally scared sick, cannot bear to see her governess ever again. And Miles . . . ?

xix. *The Harassing Teacher*

AN EXAMINATION of the governess' relationship with her charges might well begin with some consideration of her teaching. The children's uncle engages the young lady from Hampshire as governess to Flora and to Miles as well. She is to teach the latter during holidays after his term at school is over. What kind of a letter of recommendation could her employer have written for her at the end of her tour of duty at Bly?

The prose in which the twenty-four chapters of the governess' manuscript is narrated is fluent, graceful, and lucid though intricate. It leaves the reader with a wholesome respect for the intellect of its author. Ordinarily, one would suppose, the mistress of such a style should prove the ideal molder of brilliant young minds like Miles's and Flora's. Before embracing the supposition, however, one should recall that the governess who set down her experiences was not the fluttered twenty-year-old fresh from a Hampshire vicarage, but a more mature woman, a most charming person and the most agreeable woman Douglas had ever known in her position, who was years removed from Bly in time.

Besides, whether twenty or forty-five, this gifted prose stylist enjoyed the services of a remarkable amanuensis—Henry James.

To do her justice, we may as well record at once whatever seems even vaguely admirable about the governess as a teacher. It is precious little. In her narrative she is specific about her work twice. At one point we learn that she has established Flora in the schoolroom to practice making nice round O's. But we are less impressed than we might be by this no doubt salutary assignment when she reveals that she has left her pupil there and gone off to question Mrs. Grose. In the middle of the questioning, Flora appears, having abandoned paper, pencil, and copy book, expressing "in her little way an extraordinary detachment from disagreeable duties." For this dereliction she suffers, not a scolding or an additional assignment, but a wild embrace and kisses in which there is a sob of atonement.

What a disciplinarian like Dr. Arnold might have made of this pedagogical technique is not hard to imagine. In a later chapter the governess has taken Flora to play beside the lake at Bly, and "as we had lately begun geography, the lake was the Sea of Azof." These are the only details of her teaching which the governess proffers.

The rest is a dismal record of delay, indecision, confusion, neglect, ignorance, inadequacy, and injustice. In her second chapter, even before Miles, aged ten, comes home from school, before she has received the disturbing letter from his headmaster, before any apparitions trouble her at all, how does she deal with Miles's younger sister? She is frightened by her new responsibilities as well as proud of them, so that "Regular lessons, in this agitation, certainly suffered some wrong." But Flora's lot seems easy compared to that of her brother. After the headmaster's letter and Miles arrive in the second and third chapters, she finds it "simple, in my ignorance, my confusion and perhaps my conceit, to assume that I could deal with a boy whose education for the world was all on the point of beginning. . . . Lessons with me indeed, that charming summer, we all had a theory he was to have; but I now feel that for weeks the lessons must have been rather my own." Her ignorance and confusion thus begin early in the novel before her recital is an eighth of the way over or Quint and Miss Jessel intrude at all into her private torment.

Her assumption that she can cope with Miles's education is too optimistic. Yet she is unable or unwilling to propose any alternative to her own tutelage for "the end of his holidays and the resumption of his studies." In Chapter IV she finds her pupils fascinating and inspiring, but still gives no particulars concerning her instruction. Instead, she complains that both children have "a gentleness—it was their only fault, and it never made Miles a muff—that kept them . . . almost impersonal and certainly quite unpunishable." Perhaps their gentleness stood them in good stead when "There were hours, from day to day—or at least there were moments, snatched even from clear duties—when I had to shut myself up to think." Did her neglect last for hours or for moments? The reader will never know.

By Chapter VI, whether their governess is shut up in her room or actually present appears to matter little to the children: "My attention to them all really went to seeing them amuse themselves immensely without me." But they have worse things than inattention, absence, or neglect to endure. In the same chapter, "I began to watch them in a stifled suspense, a disguised tension that might well, had it continued too long, have turned to something like madness"—a teaching method which presumably both Deweyite and Arnoldist would deplore. Despite the retreats to her room, the suspense, and the tension, she displays as late as Chapter IX "an unnatural composure on the subject of another school for Miles," being "content for the time not to open the question."

The children's aptness to learn, their real brilliance ("cleverness" is the word which their awed governess continually employs), make their predicament all the more pitiable. In what may be a frantic effort to recall their teacher from her hideous introspection, both Miles and Flora perform "the dizziest feats of arithmetic, soaring quite out of *my* feeble range." My feeble range! Her sense of inadequacy is not the least of her torments. Her most striking admission comes in the ninth chapter, where she describes how Miles treats her to a "perpetually striking show of cleverness. He was too clever for a bad governess, for a parson's daughter, to spoil." After suffering one of her multifarious emotional crises, she enjoys "a queer relief . . . in the renouncement of one pretension . . . the absurdity of our prolonging the fiction that I had anything more to teach him. . . . I had had to appeal to him to let me off straining to meet him on the ground of his true capacity." Near the end of the novel she confesses to the boy himself, "Though I've renounced all claim to your company—you're so beyond me—I at least greatly enjoy it."

In spite of his gentleness, Miles does not share the governess' composure about the matter of his schooling. By Chapter XIV, when summer has gone, autumn is upon them, and the governess who is unequal to teaching him still has made no other provision for his education, he strikes. "Look here, my dear, you know . . . when in the world, please, am I going back to school?" Though he is tactful, the dialogue is nevertheless revealing:

Miles. Then when *am* I going back? . . . Of course *you* know a lot—
The Governess. But you hint that you know almost as much?
Miles. Not half I want to!

When she has still done nothing three chapters later his tact grows thin. He courageously admits that he lies awake nights thinking of "What in the world, my dear, but *you* . . . the way you bring me up." Alas that his tact and valor avail him nothing. In store for the poor lad is not a proper education, but death.

This review of the governess' career as a pedagogue at Bly scarcely prepares us for the estimate of Katherine West, herself a governess and the author of *Chapter of Governesses: A Study of the Governess in English Fiction, 1800–1949*. She pronounces James's young woman a "jolly, perfect governess" who "undertook her duties in a spirit sadly lacking in most of her kind"—that is, in a spirit of selfless service— and who possessed "the supreme gift . . . of enjoying herself with children."

But the governess' inadequacy as a teacher fades when compared to her shortcomings as a daily companion. After Mrs. Grose's plea that the governess send for the uncle, the governess becomes sure that the children are "aware of my predicament," and this awareness makes the air in which they move. By her predicament the governess means avoiding "the question of the return of the dead in general" and of the memory "of the friends little children had lost." But this is only a part of it. Her conviction that Miles and Flora and, though unseen by her, Quint and Miss Jessel, meet in her presence has already received comment. All the while, Miles and Flora must stand by willy-nilly and watch her traverse "the strange steps" of her obsession.

She gives a full account of what it drives her to. Her "exaltation"— what an appalling word for her to choose—threatens to break out into open accusations: "They're here, they're here, you little wretches . . . and you can't deny it now!" She restrains herself from doing so only because falsely accusing the innocent might prove an injury greater than what they are suffering from the demons. In other words, she is still unsure of their guilt despite her repeated protestations to the contrary. But what reader can safely accept her assurance that she manages to contain her accusations?

In the frightened state produced by Miles's "prank" she draws her "actual conclusions." These harass her so (gone, apparently, is her "recognition of all the reserves of goodness . . . he had been able to draw upon") that at odd moments she shuts herself up in her room "audibly to rehearse . . . the manner in which I might come to the point." These rehearsals—which may also be audible, alas, to Miles and Flora—are "at once a fantastic relief and a renewed despair." She flings herself about, but always breaks down "in the monstrous utterance of names." If she should pronounce them she feels she would violate the children's "instinctive delicacy." She turns crimson and covers her face with her hands as she thinks, "*They* have the manners to be silent, and you, trusted as you are, the baseness to speak!"

"After these secret scenes," which may not be so secret as she supposes, she chatters at the children "more than ever, going on volubly enough till one of our prodigious palpable hushes" occurs. During these she trembles with fear and retreats into a weird noiseless vacuum impervious to whatever noise the children may be making at the moment. The hushes, or stillnesses, absorb her despite any noise from Miles and Flora, no matter how intensified. This cheerful clamor, incidentally, reminds one of Flora's deportment immediately after or possibly during Seizure 3: the child engages in "portentous little activities by which she sought to divert my attention—the perceptible increase of movement, the greater intensity of play, the singing, the gabbling of nonsense and the invitation to romp." Does all this represent Flora's earlier effort to recall the governess to her senses?

To return to the episode above, the children's possible sufferings in the presence of one who trembles, tries tensely to avoid the subject, chatters, mentally and perhaps verbally pounds the little wretches with accusations, and retreats, now to her room to fling herself about and rehearse audibly, now into her uncanny hushes and stillnesses—their possible sufferings are not pleasant to imagine.

No one seems to have noticed how frustrating letters, including those the children write as exercises, breed additional suffering for them and constitute an interesting motif running through the novel. First there is the communication from the headmaster, its exact contents forever a mystery. Then there is the letter which the governess promises to write the uncle, but which some readers suspect never got posted. After promising, the governess only sits "for a long time before a blank sheet of paper," then goes out for a bit of prowling and a sortie into Miles's bedroom. When she tells him, "I've just begun a letter to your uncle," the long-suffering lad with more abruptness than usual says, "Well then, finish it!"

Like Mrs. Grose, Miles has difficulty in concealing his anxiety that it should get written and sent. When Mrs. Grose asks whether she has kept her promise, the governess answers yes, but fails to add that the letter, sealed and addressed, is still in her pocket. She temporizes again, reflecting that there will be "time enough to send it before the messenger should go to the village." Later, she announces that it contains "only the bare demand for an interview"; and once, before the in-

sistent eyes of Mrs. Grose, she draws the letter from her pocket, holds
it up (like some triumphant Exhibit A), and lays it on the great hall
table. "Luke will take it," she says.

In time of course she suspects Miles of taking it; instead of posting
it, "he probably will have read it and destroyed it." The conjecture is
manifestly absurd. More significant is the testimony of the not so overwrought Mrs. Grose: "Your letter won't have got there. Your letter
never went. . . . I mean that I saw yesterday, when I came back with
Miss Flora, that it wasn't where you had put it. Later in the evening I
had the chance to question Luke, and he declared that he had neither
noticed nor touched it." If neither Miles nor Luke took it, then who
did? Readers addicted to detective fiction, where it is always wise to
ponder motives, will recall to whom the letter is apt to do the most
damage should it reach Harley Street, and will suspect the governess
herself of recovering it.

Miles, then, suffers over more letters than one—the headmaster's,
the one the governess suspects him of stealing and cross-examines him
about, and those which he and Flora write in vain to their uncle. The
latter never gets mailed; the governess argues that in suppressing them
she is carrying out "the spirit of the pledge given not to appeal to
him." She also adds the wild rationalization that the children's "charming literary exercises" are "too beautiful to be posted." Thus the tan-
talizing James sees to it that their text is irrecoverable. He sees to it also
that the children are irrecoverably trapped, incommunicado.

In Chapter XVII the governess prowls noisily outside Miles's door in
the course of one of many midnight expeditions. Entering, she is in the
act of tormenting him in his bedroom, throwing herself upon him, embracing and kissing him, and gushing hysterically over him, when she
delivers several of the scores of statements which nonapparitionists find
fraught with irony. "God knows," she insists, "*I* never wished to harass him." Then directly to the boy: "I'd rather die than give you a pain
or do you a wrong—I'd rather die than hurt a hair of you." These protestations are all very well, but harass him she does, and his little sister
too. As for preferring death to causing him pain, doing him wrong, or

harming a hair on his head, it is Miles whose lot is death, from terror which she engenders. The next business of this section is to study further the general, not the final, harassment and the children's ways of dealing with it.

The governess and Mrs. Grose share the fear of what the governess calls "public accident," which means the governess' demonstrably betraying to the children her loathsome theories and her hysteria and thus plaguing them. She does so grotesquely in the scene by the lake as Seizure 7 engulfs her and, with Mrs. Grose's eyes upon her, she accuses Flora of sharing her vision of Miss Jessel's ghost. After Mrs. Grose once witnesses the kind of outburst of which the governess is capable in the children's presence, she acts at once. The jig is up. As the governess puts it, in language that contrasts oddly with her usual precise, elegant, patrician style, "I *did* put my foot in it! She'll [Flora will] never speak to me again!"

Another public accident transpires enroute to church in Chapter XIV when Miles presses her on the subject of arranging properly for him to resume his education. She makes an hysterical effort to avoid the issue by quickening their steps. She seems "literally to be running a race," which Miles wins. Since they are within sight of the church, where various people, including several of the staff at Bly, are clustered to watch them go in, she obviously makes a public spectacle of herself. An additional comment from Miles makes her "literally . . . bound forward" until he imposes a halt on her "by the pressure of his arm."

His next question makes her "drop straight down" onto a low, table-like tomb. By this time Mrs. Grose, Flora, and the other worshipers have entered the church; one hopes they cannot see from the windows the governess' astonishing performance. Miles threatens to send for his uncle and marches off alone into the church. At first the governess only sits on the tomb and surrenders to agitation. But then her "deep discomposure" drives her "round the church, hesitating, hovering," and considering flight. If visible in the church, especially as she pauses beneath the east window with the light behind her and listens to the service, she must have taken many a mind off the sermon.

With her "ugly and queer" face, she could well have induced through the window a mass shock of the kind Quint gave her in Seizure 2. If not—well, the rest of her performance has constituted an accident sufficiently public. From Mrs. Grose's point of view, it is limited in its heinousness, however, because it involves only peculiar behavior and not the betrayal of gruesome theories about evil spirits. Even so, it is enough to account for Mrs. Grose's prompt change in attitude.

So much for the public accidents Mrs. Grose has an opportunity to judge for herself. Now, what of the private ones that are private only in the sense that they are not immediately known to Mrs. Grose though all the while the children may be experiencing their terror? Carried away by the general torrent of words, apparitionists have overlooked the truth of the matter contained in two small speeches, one by Miles and one by Flora. When during Seizure 7 the governess hurls into Flora's face the fantastic charge, Miss Jessel is "there, you little unhappy thing —there, there, *there*, and you know it as well as you know me," Flora replies, "I don't know what you mean. I see nobody. I see nothing. I never *have*. I think you're cruel. I don't like you!"

Marius Bewley is surely right in saying that "I never *have*" gives us some idea of all the children must have been through at the governess' hands. The child's emphatic denial proves, of course, that the governess' accusation is not new to Flora. When, where, and how often the governess has given voice to it may not be determinable, but we can and in a moment will point out the likeliest places. One thing Flora's denial does *not* prove is that the governess has also previously brought out the awful names of the departed, though it may not seem much of a consolation for her to have left the accusations vague. At any rate, as she produces the name of Miss Jessel now, she adds, "Much as I had made of the fact that this name had never once, between us, been sounded, the quick smitten glare with which the child's face now received it fairly likened my breach of the silence to the smash of a pane of glass."

Miles's revealing remark is a preamble to the gruelling bedroom scene already treated. As the governess, "under my endless obsession," stands listening at his door, he calls out gaily, "I say, you there—come in." Like Mrs. Grose, on other occasions, he tries to introduce a light touch into his nursing. "Well, what are *you* up to?" he inquires. When she asks how he knew she was there, he replies, laughing, "Why of course I heard you. Did you fancy you made no noise? You're like a troop of cavalry!" Note the force of the present tense, "You *are* like a troop of cavalry," suggesting habitual clamor in the corridors and who knows where else when the governess is convinced she is silence itself.

Miles's concern for her is deep. He lies awake and thinks about her, he confesses—"of this queer business of ours . . . the way you bring me up. And all the rest!" How pointed "this queer business" and "all the rest" seem, once the reader is aware that the children know of her sleeplessness, her endless insane forays into the night, and her grievances—though probably as yet imperfectly defined—against them.

Armed with this knowledge, one finds many of Miles's speeches which have hitherto seemed ambiguous or cryptic replete with significance. Ponder Miles's plaintive questions, "Does my uncle think what *you* think? . . . I mean does *he* know?" In a brief discussion of his schooling, the governess states, "I thought you wanted to go on as you are." The vehemence of his reply may have startled her: "I don't—I don't. I want to get away."

The Governess. You want to go to your uncle?
Miles. Ah you can't get off with that!
The Governess. My dear, I don't want to get off!
Miles. You can't, even if you do. You can't, you can't! My uncle must come down, and you must completely settle things.
The Governess. If we do, you may be sure it will be to take you quite away.
Miles. Well, don't you understand that that's exactly what I'm working for? You'll have to tell him—about the way you've let it all [our present tutelage and the decision about my future schooling?] drop: you'll have to tell him a tremendous lot!

The eloquence of the "tremendous lot," the dash after "You'll have to tell him," and "you must completely settle things" will not be lost on the reader with an inkling of what the children have been enduring.

xx. *Nurses for the Grimacing, Shrieking Gaoler*

HOW MUCH, one wonders, does the governess enjoy what John Lydenberg calls her "unrelenting surveillance" of the children? Her own attestation to its relentlessness is conclusive, as a few of the pertinent phrases from the text (presented in chronological order) will show: "in these weeks that I myself have lived with him [Miles] and so closely watched him"; "they make me feel more than ever that I must watch"; "in constant sight of my pupils"; "I was careful almost never to be out of" the children's company; "the rigour with which I kept my pupils in sight"; "Why did they never resent my inexorable, my perpetual society? . . . I had all but pinned the boy to my shawl. . . . I was like a gaoler with an eye to possible surprises and escapes"; "his eternal governess"; "it was the very first time [the governess writes as late as Chapter XVIII] I had allowed the little girl out of my sight without some special provision."

She may be said in a sense to enjoy all this self-imposed sentry duty as part of Doing Her Duty, heroically keeping watch over her charges and fending off demons. But how about Miles and Flora? What enjoyment does this kind of concentration-camp surveillance bring them?

The answer, in Chapter XVII, could not be plainer. The "gaoler," who has come to his room for one of her very late, nocturnal visits (tours of inspection might be a more accurate description) asks, "Is there nothing —nothing at all that you want to tell me?" He replies, "I've told you—I told you this morning [that I want to go back to school]." With more than her usual perception she now inquires, "That you just want me not to worry you?" And he says, "To let me alone." Could any reply be more concise or clear than these four words?

In the next chapter Miles underscores his stand by his tactful, magnanimous treatment of her in a fashion "tantamount to his saying outright: 'The true knights we love to read about never push an advantage too far. I know what you mean now: you mean that—to be let alone yourself and not followed up—you'll cease to worry and spy upon me, won't keep me so close to you, will let me go and come'."

The inexorable, perpetual society even of a saint would pall after months, but at least such a companion, exuding an odor of sanctity, would be eternally wreathed in smiles and giving tongue to the sweetest and most beatific of melodies. The governess, on the contrary, has no such sights and sounds to offer her prisoners, or Mrs. Grose either. Harold C. Goddard was the first to call attention to the insane looks and noises to which she treats her household, and one can do no better than repeat his examples and augment them with a few more.

"I was conscious as I spoke that I looked prodigious things, for I got the slow reflexion of them in my companion's face."

Miss Jessel "only fixed the child . . . with such awful eyes!" Mrs. Grose "stared at mine as if they might really have resembled them."

The Governess. "I don't wonder you looked queer." *Mrs. Grose.* "I doubt if I looked as queer as you!"

"I seemed to see in the beautiful face with which he [Miles] watched me how ugly and queer I looked."

The Governess. "Did I look very queer?" *Mrs. Grose.* "Dreadful!"

Mrs. Grose. "What in the name of goodness is the matter—?" *The*

Governess. "With me?" I must have made a wonderful face. "Do I show it?" *Mrs. Grose.* "You're as white as a sheet. You look awful."

Flora "had looked at me in sweet speculation and then had accused me to my face of having 'cried.' I had supposed the ugly signs of it brushed away."

"I quickly rose and I think I must have shown her a queerer face than ever yet."

"I was queer company enough—quite as queer as the company I received."

"I must have shown her—as I was indeed but too conscious—a front of miserable defeat."

"My heart . . . leaped into my mouth. *Would* he [Miles] tell me why? I found no sound on my lips to press it, and I was aware of answering only with a vague repeated grimacing nod. He was gentleness itself, and while I wagged my head at him . . ."

In the children's presence "I had perpetually . . . to check the irrelevant gaze and discouraged sigh."

Sighs are the least nerve-wracking sounds she emits. The oceans of tears she sheds are often accompanied by sobs, of which Mrs. Grose is the principal auditor, though the children are by no means spared them altogether. In addition, as Goddard says, her "insane laugh, as well as her insane look, is frequently alluded to. . . . of references to her maniacal cries there are several: 'I had to smother a kind of howl,' she says. . . . Or again, when she catches Miss Jessel sitting at her table: 'I heard myself break into a sound that, by the open door, rang through the long passage and the empty house'."

Maybe some day an enterprising scholar with plenty of time and patience will make a thorough study of the governess' laughter. He might entitle his article, irreverently, "Henry James's Laughing Girl." For the moment we take time and space to observe only that laughing when there is really nothing to laugh at is said to be, in the young, a symptom of hebephrenia, itself a prelude to dementia praecox. We might furthermore point the way by offering a handful of cogent specimens from the text: "with a laugh, a little silly doubtless to match her own"; " 'Oh I've no pretensions,' I could laugh"; " 'He has an odd way —it comes over me now,' I laughed"; "I broke in with a laugh that was doubtless significant"; "to gain time, I tried to laugh." And on and on through the murky corridors at Bly she makes her laughing way.

Mrs. Grose, as we have shown, frequently serves as an attendant to this victim of hebephrenia. But who is to tend her in the housekeeper's absence? In the scene where Miles threatens to send for his uncle and precipitate an accounting from the governess, he may be employing the same kind of shock tactics Mrs. Grose uses when she also threatens the patient with sending for their employer. This possibility brings us to what, according to the nonapparitionist reading, is the crowning irony of the tale. Mrs. Grose is not alone in her nursing. Without the housekeeper's knowledge, those whom the governess is employed to care for are obliged to care for her instead. They are tireless and valiant in their exertions as they try to help her regain her balance. With "a great deal of tacit arrangement," but never with tongue in cheek or vulgarity, they set about their task.

They show "a delightful endless appetite for passages in my own history," which she willingly reiterates. Urging her on to autobiographical recitations represents a nursing technique not mentioned before. It is presumably efficacious (she finds Miles's endless curiosity "delightful") since they employ it extensively, pulling "with an art of their own the strings of my invention and my memory." One thinks again of the psychiatrist's couch, upon which they seem metaphorically to have deposited the patient to pour out "the story of my smallest adventure," along with anecdotes about her brothers, sisters, whimsical father, the family cat and dog and clever pony, the furniture and arrangement of the vicarage. Where the governess sees not "the least pertinence" and "no visible connexion" in their breaking out "into sociable reminders" and inviting her "to repeat afresh" her little anecdotes, the nonapparitionist detects relevance and design. The children have hit on still another "treatment" they hope will work.

They do not, however, abandon other means tried, maybe with partial success, in the past. When the governess hurls her cruel charge (aloud this time, or still mental?), "They're here, they're here, you little wretches . . . and you can't deny it now," the wretches *do* deny it "with all the added volume of their sociability and their tenderness," and they apparently strive in vain with "intensified mirth or quickened recitation or louder strum of the piano" to dissipate the hushes and stillnesses into which she retires. Also as in the past, they kiss her "inveterately with a wild irrelevance," but if such demonstrations of affection have soothed her earlier, they are *not* irrelevant. Why not try them again?

Sometimes the little nurses appear to seek relief from the tension of coping with their patient who is everlastingly present. They contrive "to let me alone without appearing to drop me and to accompany me without appearing to oppress." They "amuse themselves immensely without me: this was a spectacle they seemed actively to prepare and that employed me as an active admirer. I walked in a world of their invention—they had no occasion whatever to draw upon mine." In other words, at times the children are making a life for themselves in which they kindly include their ailing governess.

As if they were physicians trying to control some vaguely diagnosed and imperfectly understood disease by running the gamut of the new miracle drugs, Miles and Flora try yet another tack in this phase of the governess' derangement. After the inveterate kisses one or the other never fails to pose certain questions found by experience effective for helping them "through many a peril . . . for carrying off an awkwardness." The questions are, "When do you think he [our uncle] *will* come? Don't you think we *ought* to write?" They live "in much profusion of theory that he might at any moment arrive to mingle in our circle." Were they characters in an opera by Puccini instead of in a novel by James, either Miles or Flora would sing in this scene "Un bel di vedremo."

Like Mrs. Grose, they seem to apprehend the root of their patient's troubles and strike at it. They get "into such splendid training" at dealing with seizures that "each time, to mark the close of the incident," they go "almost automatically through the very same movements." The unvarying ritual includes the kisses, the questions about the uncle, and the actual writing of letters to him by the children. These, the governess lets them understand, are but charming literary exercises. She finds them "too beautiful to be posted," keeps them herself, and has them still in her possession decades later when she writes out her narrative.

What a pity she does not quote some of them; they might make interesting reading. It would be surprising if they did not contain some reflection of the children's need for deliverance—even *very* urgent pleas for a visit. At the same time, the governess finds them beautiful, maybe because they overflow with lavish encomiums for her: possibly more therapeutics administered by her nurses. She also seems to see in the letters a threat, and she may be right: "It was exactly as if our young friends knew how almost more awkward than anything else" would be their uncle's appearance at Bly.

All the while the patient is so selfishly engrossed in her own "fine machinery" to attract the uncle's attention to her slighted charms that she fails to realize, let alone appreciate, what the children are up to.

"I used to wonder," the governess writes, "how my little charges could help guessing that I thought strange things about them." The truth is of course that they do not have to guess; they *know*. "I trembled lest they should see that they *were* so immensely more interesting." They know all about this disquieting immense interest; their immediate problem is to cope with the trembling.

James concentrates many of the pathetic details of their ordeal in a single chapter, Chapter IX:

There were moments when I knew myself to catch them up by an irresistible impulse and press them to my heart. As soon as I had done so I used to wonder: "What will they think of that? Doesn't it betray too much?" It would have been easy to get into a sad wild tangle about how much I might betray. . . . if it occurred to me that I might occasionally excite suspicion by the little outbreaks of my sharper passion for them, so too I remember asking if I mightn't see a queerness in the traceable increase of their own demonstrations.

Again, "They were at this period extravagantly and preternaturally fond of me; which, after all, I could reflect, was no more than a grace-ful response in children perpetually bowed down over and hugged." Had she been less self-centered, she could have seen in their demonstra-tions a great deal more than a "graceful response." She might have re-flected that they were using their only resources—their tact, sympathy, concern, and love for her—to nurse her back to sanity. To overlook the fact that, like Mrs. Grose, the children too love the governess deeply is to miss one of the most poignant facets of the story.

A review of their efforts in her behalf is heartbreaking. They have never "wanted to do so many things for their poor protectress." They get their lessons better and better. They divert, entertain, and surprise her; read her passages, tell her stories, act out charades; pounce out at her disguised as animals and historical characters—tigers, Romans, Shakespeareans, astronomers, and navigators. They astonish her by re-citing interminable pieces secretly got by heart, "unimposed little miracles of memory."

The governess confesses that their piano playing breaks into "all gruesome fancies." Apparently they are able to experiment with a kind of treatment not available to Mrs. Grose—musical therapy. When that fails to bring the patient round, Miles and Flora confer in corners and try another tack, one retiring in high spirits to "come in" as something new.

Despite anxieties and fruitless efforts, Miles and Flora never quar-rel or complain. Sometimes, when the governess drops "into coarse-ness," she apprehends "little understandings between them by which one of them should keep me occupied while the other slipped away." Does Miles encourage Flora to depart and so escape the governess' coarseness, or are they like two nurses relieving one another in shifts? They implement their understandings "with the minimum of gross-ness." After a lull the grossness breaks out "all in the other quarter," meaning we suppose in herself. How extraordinary that the prim gov-erness should thus confess to her own coarseness and grossness. Where on earth did she learn them, if linguistic? Surely not in the Hampshire vicarage—unless from the brothers upon whom, she tells us, she dotes.

Perhaps at Bly she could have been reading *Tom Jones* as well as *Amelia*. Whatever the source, it does not seem to deter the children's exertions. They love her, try to care for her, never appear indifferent to her suffering.

The coarseness and grossness require further comment, for they may explain one of the cruxes of the story. After Flora's deliverance from the unquiet bedroom she has had to share with the governess for too long, she passes the night with her trusty old friend Mrs. Grose. Because of the constant vigilance of the governess, this is probably the first chance the child, now "markedly feverish," has enjoyed to tell the housekeeper a thing or two about night life in the upper reaches of Bly. Very early the next morning Mrs. Grose comes to the governess' room and admits that Flora has told her really shocking things about the governess—"horrors," "beyond everything, for a young lady."

Has Flora been telling Mrs. Grose about the dreadful nights she has shared with the governess, nights empty of sleep but full of prowling, or about days in the schoolroom made dreadful by the governess' spells and by difficult nursing chores, or about accusations that the governess supposes she has suppressed but has made all too vocal, or about physical violence from the governess with her spasmodic gripping of her little charge?

Mrs. Grose cannot imagine "wherever she must have picked up—" but never gets to finish the sentence, the governess interrupting: "The appalling language she applies to me? I can then!" The governess means—and apparitionists would agree with her—that Miss Jessel's hold over Flora has ruined the child's vocabulary as well as her morals. Mrs. Grose's next comment, however, suggests that she has in mind some of the ranting to which the governess has generously treated her, and apparently Flora too, in the past: "Well, perhaps I ought to also—since I've heard some of it before!"

To meet Seizure 4 the governess goes straight out of the room she shares with Flora and from the hall "noiselessly" closes and locks the door. What effect being deserted in the middle of the night and locked in might produce on her roommate she does not pause to consider. The seizure over, she returns and finds to her terror that Flora is not in her bed and that the bed curtains have been "deceivingly" pulled forward. The child almost immediately appears from behind the window blind. Her being at the window suggests that she may have been looking for the governess outside because prowling the grounds was, like some of Lady Macbeth's behavior, an accustomed action with the governess in the throes of a seizure. Flora looks "intensely grave"—and addresses the governess "with a reproach. 'You naughty: where *have* you been'."

Yet there is remarkable tact and sweetness in what the child does and says in this crisis. She explains that she "had known, suddenly, as she lay there, that I was out of the room, and had jumped up to see what had become of me," which may be a kind way of saying, "You woke me up again when you went out and closed and locked the door."

The Governess. You were looking for me out of the window? You thought I might be walking in the grounds?
Flora. Well, you know, I thought someone was.
The Governess. And did you see anyone?
Flora. Ah *no*!
The Governess. Why did you pull the curtain over the place to make me think you were still there?
Flora. Because I don't like to frighten you!
The Governess. But if I had, by your idea, gone out—?
Flora. Oh but you know that you might come back, you dear, and that you *have*!

In this scene Flora has to deal with the patient's actions as well as her words, and her postseizural behavior frequently turns violent. At eight years of age, the child is unable to avail herself of Mrs. Grose's technique of pinioning the hands. When the governess drops into a chair "with the joy of her reappearance" and feels faint, Flora patters straight over to her and throws herself upon her governess' knee "to be held." The governess closes her eyes an instant but then glares at the girl—"Oh how I looked at her now!"

Closing her eyes again, she believes absolutely that Flora is lying to her and ponders "three or four possible ways in which I might take this up." One of these tempts her "with such singular intensity that, to resist it, I must have gripped my little girl with a spasm that, wonderfully, she submitted to without a cry or a sign of fright." Next, she springs to her feet. At last, Flora gets back to her bed, where for "a long time" the governess rounds out the session "by almost sitting on her for the retention of her hand."

What a grim fate for an eight-year-old girl: to be awakened by her prowling "patient"; to find her gone; to look vainly for her in the grounds; to watch her turn faint, drop into a chair, alternately close her eyes and glare, then spring to her feet; to be gripped spasmodically and no doubt painfully; to be almost sat upon for a long time to have her hand held. Most terrible of all is the possibility raised by what is going through the governess' mind while she does the spasmodic gripping. Believing unconditionally that the child is lying, the governess is tempted with "singular intensity" to "break out at her on the spot and have it all over."

"Why not . . . give it to her straight in her lovely little lighted face. 'You see, you see, you *know* that you do and that you already quite suspect I believe it; therefore why not frankly confess it to me, so that we may at least live with it together and learn perhaps, in the strangeness of our fate, where we are and what it means?' "

Instead of succumbing to the temptation, the governess leaps to her feet, and the tirade "dropped, alas, as it came." Or so she fondly believes. The reader cannot be sure in the light of Flora's later outburst at the lake: "I think you're cruel. I don't like you" seems all too apt a sequel to the scene just reviewed. Is this the point in the governess' derangement when her accusations become vocal?

The violence of the children's ultimate revulsion against the governess provides an index to the extent of the suffering she has caused them. Flora's "Take me away, take me away—oh take me away from *her*" is exceeded in desperation only by an even more terse cry Miles utters in his death scene.

Readers who are unconvinced that the governess literally frightens Miles to death should review this scene, the last in the novel, paying special attention to the sights and sounds she subjects the child to. "My voice trembled so that I felt it impossible to suppress the shake," she writes early in the scene, but already he is growing "more and more visibly nervous." Then as she lapses into her eighth and final seizure, she enfolds him "with a moan of joy." Next, " 'And [in my letter you stole] you found nothing. . . . Nothing, nothing!' I almost shouted in my joy." He draws "his breath, two or three times over, as if with difficulty." He fetches up "a deep-drawn sigh" and, though he manages to put some distance between them, he is "still breathing hard." He is also sweating from every pore; his forehead is drenched.

His agony fails to deter her: "with a single bound and an irrepressible cry" she springs "straight upon him." Miles is panting. Still she tries to press him against her. " 'No more, no more, no more!' I shrieked." His head gives "a frantic little shake for air and light," his face gives "round the room, its convulsed supplication," he jerks straight around, stares, glares, and then, with a cry of his own, he dies. He has seen one hideous sight, felt one smothering embrace, and heard one terrifying theory, sigh, sob, moan, shout, cry, and shriek too many.

Amid the horrifying sounds, he asks whether Miss Jessel is present, a question which his tormentor recognizes (correctly) as "some sequel to what we had done to Flora." She forces him to say, "It's *he*?" and icily inquires, "Whom do you mean by 'he'?" His last words on earth are "Peter Quint—you devil! *Where*?" About this speech there has been much dispute, the governess and apparitionists contending that "you devil" signalizes Miles's final recognition of the demon's wickedness, and "his tribute to my devotion." Nonapparitionists, staggered by the irony of her misconstruction, wonder how anyone could doubt that the phrase which he flings into her face with his dying breath is meant to indict *her*—the grimacing, shrieking goaler from whom he is about to escape at last.

In the year the novel was published James wrote Louis Waldstein, "But ah, the exposure indeed, the helpless plasticity of childhood that isn't dear or sacred to *somebody*! That *was* my little tragedy." In the light or rather the gloom (as the governess would say) of the evidence reviewed in this study, we cannot agree with Oliver Evans that "without the apparitions there is no evil, no danger, and no *exposure*." The children suffer prolonged, helpless, lethally dangerous exposure to the mad governess. As Osborn Andreas says, she "is really engulfing them into the vortex of her hallucinatory world." Their exposure ends only when Flora lies delirious and Miles lies dead in the governess' arms, both victims of her endless harassment and of mortal terror.

A SELECTED BIBLIOGRAPHY

A SELECTED BIBLIOGRAPHY

The following symbols and abbreviations indicate various evaluations of the contents of the books and articles cited in the bibliography:

A Apparitionist approach
Am Ambiguity in *The Turn of the Screw*
B Biographical details concerning the governess
Bio Possible Jamesian biographical significance
Cf *The Turn of the Screw* compared to other fiction
Do The governess' doubts about her sanity
Dr Comments by drama critics: stage, movies, television, or opera
Em The governess' emotional needs, avidity
F Flora
Ge General critical comments
Go The governess
Gr Mrs. Grose
H The bachelor uncle of Harley Street
Ha The question of hallucinations or delusions
Ho The horror induced by *The Turn of the Screw*
I Illustrations (graphic) of *The Turn of the Screw*
J Miss Jessel
Ln Leans toward nonapparitionism
M Miles
N Nonapparitionist approach
Na The names in *The Turn of the Screw*
O Origins, or sources, of *The Turn of the Screw*
P The governess' passion for H
Psy Psychological approach, Freudian or otherwise
Pv Point of view
S Praise in superlative terms
St The prose style
T The governess as teacher
Te Technique
Th Theological or philosophical approach
U Uncomplimentary critiques

Anderson, Quentin, "The American Henry James," Doctoral Dissertation, Columbia University, 1953, pp. 188–189. *F Go H J M P Psy Th*

Andreas, Osborn, *Henry James and the Expanding Horizon*, Seattle, University of Washington Press, 1948, pp. 46–47, 50. *Em F Ge Ha N T*

Archibald, William, *The Innocents: A New Play . . . Based on "The Turn of the Screw,"* New York, Coward-McCann, Inc., 1950, pp. x, 78. *A I*

Arnavon, Cyrille, *Les lettres américaines devant la critique française*, Paris, Société d'édition des belles lettres, 1951, p. 92. *Ge*

Arvin, Newton, "Henry James and the Almighty Dollar," *The Hound and Horn*, VII, 3 (April–May 1934), 434–443. *Cf Ge U*

Athenaeum, The, "Mr. James's New Stories," No. 3704 (October 22, 1898), pp. 564–565. *Ho St Te*

Atkinson, Brooks, "First Night at the Theatre," *The New York Times*, XCIX, 33,612, February 2, 1950, p. 30. *Dr Ge St*

Baker, Ernest A., *The History of the English Novel: The Day before Yesterday*, London, H. F. & G. Witherby, Ltd., 1938, IX, 254–255. *F Ho J M Te Q*

Barnes, Howard, *New York Theatre Critics' Reviews 1950*, XI, 4 (February 6, 1950), 360. *A Am D Ge*

Barzun, Jacques, "Henry James, Melodramatist," *The Question of Henry James*, ed. F. W. Dupee, New York, Henry Holt and Co., 1945, p. 261. *A Cf*

Beach, Joseph Warren, "Henry James," *Cambridge History of American Literature*, II, New York, G. P. Putnam's Sons, 1921, 104. *Ge S*

——— *The Method of Henry James*, Philadelphia, Albert Saifer, 1954, pp. lii, 185. *F Ge Go J M Q*

——— *The Twentieth Century Novel*, New York, The Century Company, 1932, pp. 204, 208–209, 344. *Cf Ho Pv Te*

Beckley, Paul V., "The New Movie: 'The Innocents'," New York *Herald Tribune*, December 26, 1961, p. 9. *A Dr Go Ho M Psy*

Bedford, Sybille, "Fantasy without Whimsy" (a review of Muriel Spark's *The Go-Away Bird and Other Stories*), *Saturday Review*, XLIII, 47 (November 19, 1960), 29. *Cf*

Beer, Thomas, "Henry James and Stephen Crane," *The Question of Henry James*, ed. F. W. Dupee, New York, Henry Holt and Co., 1945, pp. 105–107. *F J M Q*

Beerbohm, Max. See Behrman, S. N.

Beers, Henry A., "Fifty Years of Hawthorne," *Yale Review*, IV, 2 (January 1915), 307. *Cf Ln*

Behrman, S. N., "Conversation with Max," *The New Yorker*, XXXVI, 2, (February 27, 1960), 88–89. *A Ha*

Benson, E. F., *As We Were: A Victorian Peep Show*, London, Longmans, Green and Co., 1930, pp. 278–279. *F Ge J O Q S*

Berland, Alwyn, "The Complex Fate," *The Sewanee Review*, LXI, 2 (Spring 1953), 326. *Cf H*

Bewley, Marius, "Appearance and Reality in Henry James," *Scrutiny*, XVII, 2 (Summer 1950), 104, 106–107, 109–111. *Em F Go Gr H Ha J M N Na Q T*

———— *The Complex Fate*, New York, Grove Press, 1954, pp. 132–143. *F Go M N*

———— "Correspondence: The Relation between William and Henry James," *Scrutiny*, XVII, 4 (March 1951), 331–334. *Ge Go Te Th*

———— *The Eccentric Design*, New York, Columbia University Press, 1959, p. 253. *Ge*

———— "Maisie, Miles and Flora, the Jamesian Innocents," *Scrutiny*, XVII, 3 (Autumn 1950), 258. *F Go M N*

Birkhead, Edith, *The Tale of Terror*, New York, E. P. Dutton & Co., 1921, p. 196. *Ge Ho Psy*

Blackmur, Richard P., "The Critical Prefaces," *The Hound and Horn*, VII, 3 (April–May 1934), 459. *A J Q*

———— "The Sphinx and the Housecat," *Accent*, VI, 1 (Autumn 1945), 62. *Am U*

Bosanquet, Theodora, "Henry James," *The Fortnightly Review*, CVII (June 1917), 996. *Ho*

Bowen, Elizabeth, *English Novelists*, London, William Collins, 1946, p. 42. *Ge Th*

Brewster, Dorothy, *Modern Fiction* (with John Angus Burrell), New York, Columbia University Press, 1935, p. 403. *Ge S*

Bronson, Walter C., *A History of American Literature*, New York, D. C. Heath and Co., 1919, pp. 303–304. *Ge Ho*

Brooks, Van Wyck, *The Pilgrimage of Henry James*, New York, E. P. Dutton and Co., 1925, pp. 140, 150. *Am Bio J S T*

Broun, Heywood, Introduction to James's *The Turn of the Screw*, New York, The Modern Library, 1930, pp. v–ix. *Ge Ho S*

Brown, John Mason, "Seeing Things," *The Saturday Review*, February 25, 1950, pp. 32–36. *Am Dr Ge H Ha Ho Ja Ln St*

Brownell, W. C., *American Prose Masters*, New York, Charles Scribner's Sons, 1923, p. 355. *Ge U*

Burke, Kenneth, *A Rhetoric of Motives,* New York, Prentice-Hall, Inc., 1950, pp. 116–117, 215. *Bio J Ja Psy Q*

Burrell, John Angus. See Brewster, Dorothy.

Cameron, Kate, "Criterion Presents Classic Ghost Story," New York *Daily News,* December 26, 1961, p. 48. *Dr F Go Gr H Ho J Ln M Psy Q*

Cargill, Oscar, "Henry James as Freudian Pioneer," *Chicago Review,* X, 2 (Summer 1956), 13–29. *Am Bio Ha Ja O*

——— *The Novels of Henry James,* New York, The Macmillan Co., 1961, pp. 260, 261, 480, 489. *Ge*

Cary, Elisabeth Luther, "Henry James," *Scribner's Magazine,* XXXVI, 4 (October 1904), 394–400. *Ho*

Castellanos, Rosario, "El fin de la inocencia," *Revista de la Universidad de Mexico,* VII (July 1963), 4–7. *A Am F Go H I J M Pv S Th*

Chapman, John, *New York Theatre Critics' Reviews 1950,* XI, 4 (February 6, 1950), 359. *Dr Ge*

Chesterton, G. K., *The Victorian Age in Literature,* London, Oxford University Press, 1955, p. 141. *Ge S*

Chislett, William, Jr., *Moderns and Near-Moderns,* New York, The Grafton Press, 1928, pp. 40, 61. *A F Go J M Q*

Clurman, Harold, "Theatre: Change of Mood," *The New Republic,* CXXII, 9 (February 27, 1950), 20–21. *Bio Dr*

Coleman, Robert, *New York Theatre Critics' Reviews 1950,* XI, 4 (February 6, 1950), 360. *Dr Ge U*

Collins, Carvel, "James' *The Turn of the Screw,*" *The Explicator,* XIII, 8 (June 1955), Item 49. *B F Go Gr H Ha Ja M N*

Cook, Alton, "Oldtime Ghost Tale," New York *World-Telegram,* December 26, 1961, p. 15. *Dr Em F Go Ho J M Psy Q St*

Cowie, Alexander, *The Rise of the American Novel,* New York, American Book Co., 1948, pp. 719, 720. *S*

Cowley, Malcolm, "The Return of Henry James," *The New Republic,* CXII, 4 (January 22, 1945), 121–122. *Ge S*

——— "The Two Henry Jameses," *The New Republic,* CXII, 1575 (February 5, 1945), 177. *S*

Critic, The, XXXIII, 858 (December 1898), 523–524. *Ge Go Ho Ln S*

Crowther, Bosley, "Screen: 'The Innocents'," *The New York Times,* December 26, 1961, p. 15. *Em F Go H Ha Ho M N Psy*

Daiches, David, "Sensibility and Technique," *Kenyon Review,* V, 4 (Autumn 1943), 571–572, 576. *A Ge H*

De Blois, Frank, "A Part for Miss Bergman," *TV Guide,* VII, 42 (October 17, 1959), 17–19. *Am Dr F Ge Go M*

De la Mare, Walter, "Henry James," *The Living Age,* Eighth Series, II, 3744 (April 8, 1916), 122–125. *Ho St*

Derleth, August, *Writing Fiction,* Boston, The Writer, Inc., 1946, pp. 101, 114. *Ge S*

De Voto, Bernard, *The World of Fiction,* Boston, Houghton Mifflin Co., 1950, pp. 213–214. *Ge Psy Te*

Dickinson, Thomas H., *The Making of American Literature,* New York, The Century Co., 1932, p. 585. *Ge*

Dictionary of American Biography, ed. Dumas Malone, New York, Charles Scribner's Sons, 1933, IX, 583. *Ge*

Dolmatch, Theodore B., "Edmund Wilson as Literary Critic," *The University of Kansas City Review,* XVII, 3 (Spring 1951), 213–219. *Am Bio Ja Psy*

Dupee, F. W., *Henry James: His Life and Writings,* Garden City, Doubleday and Co., Inc., 1956, pp. 151, 159–160. *Am Do Em F Go Gr J Ja Ha Ln M Q*

—— *The Question of Henry James,* New York, Henry Holt and Company, 1945, p. xv. *Bio Psy*

Dyne, Michael, *The Others,* National Broadcasting Company Matinee Theatre, February 15, 1957. A dramatization of the tale.

Edel, Leon, "The Architecture of Henry James's 'New York Edition'," *New England Quarterly,* XXIV, 2 (June 1951), 169–178. *Ja*

—— "The Enduring Fame of Henry James," *The New York Times Book Review,* September 3, 1961, pp. 1, 16. *Ge Psy St*

—— *The Ghostly Tales of Henry James,* New Brunswick, Rutgers University Press, 1948, pp. v–xxxii, 425–435. *Am B F Go H Ho J Ja M N O*

—— "Hugh Walpole and Henry James: The Fantasy of the 'Killer and the Slain'," *The American Imago,* VIII, 4 (December 1951), 3–21. *B Cf Em Go H M N P Psy Q U*

—— "Letters to the Editors," *The Times Literary Supplement,* No. 2458, March 12, 1949, p. 169. *Ja*

—— "The Literary Convictions of Henry James," *Modern Fiction Studies,* III, 1 (Spring 1957), 3–10. *F Go Gr J M N Q*

—— *The Psychological Novel, 1900–1950,* New York, J. B. Lippincott Co., 1955, pp. 59–68. *B F Go Gr J M N P Q Te*

Edgar, Pelham, *Henry James: Man and Author,* London, Grant Richards, Ltd., 1927, pp. 188–189. *F Ge Go Gr Ho J M Q S*

Egan, Maurice Francis, "The Revelation of an Artist in Literature," *The Catholic World*, CXI, 663 (June 1920), 293. *Cf F Ho M S*

Eliot, T. S., "Henry James," *The Shock of Recognition*, ed. Edmund Wilson, New York, Farrar, Strauss and Cudahy, 1955, pp. 856, 862. *Ge*

———— "On Henry James," *The Question of Henry James*, ed. F. W. Dupee, New York, Henry Holt and Co., 1945, pp. 110, 116. *Cf Psy Te*

Elton, Oliver, *Modern Studies*, London, Edward Arnold, 1907, pp. 255–256. *F Go H Ha Ho J Ln M Pv Q*

Evans, Oliver, "James's Air of Evil: 'The Turn of the Screw'," *Partisan Review*, XVI, 2 (February 1949), 175–187. *A Go Gr J Ja Q*

Fadiman, Clifton, "The Revival of Interest in Henry James," *The New York Herald Tribune Weekly Book Review*, XXI, 21 (January 14, 1945), 1–2. *Ge Th*

————, ed., *The Short Stories of Henry James*, New York, Random House, 1945, pp. x–xi, xii–xiii, xv–xvi. *Bio Psy S Te Th*

Fagin, N. B., "Another Reading of *The Turn of the Screw*," *MLN*, LVI, 3 (March 1941), 196–202. *A F Go H J Ja M Q*

Falk, Robert P., "Henry James and the 'Age of Innocence'," *Nineteenth-Century Fiction*, VII, 3 (December 1952), 171–188. *F J M Psy Q Te Th*

Fay, Gerard, "Review of *The Innocents*," *Spectator*, No. 6472 (July 11, 1952), 65. *Dr Ge M Te*

Fiedler, Leslie A., *No! In Thunder*, Boston, Beacon Press, 1960, p. 286.

Firebaugh, Joseph J., "Inadequacy in Eden: Knowledge and 'The Turn of the Screw'," *Modern Fiction Studies*, III, 1 (Spring 1957), 57–63. *A Cf F Go Gr H Ha J Ja M Psy Q T Th*

Foley, Richard Nicholas, *Criticism in American Periodicals of the Works of Henry James from 1866 to 1916*, Washington, D.C., The Catholic University of America Press, 1944, pp. 72–73. *Ge S*

Follett, Wilson, "Henry James and the Untold Story," *The Dial*, LXIII, 755 (December 6, 1917), 580. *Cf Ge*

———— *The Modern Novel*, New York, Alfred A. Knopf, 1923, pp. 306, 315. *Ge St*

Ford, Ford Madox, *Henry James: A Critical Study*, New York, Albert and Charles Boni, 1915, pp. 121, 146–147, 151, 156, 169. *Am F Ge H Ho J Ja M Q S St*

———— "The Master," *The London Mercury*, XXXIII, 193 (November 1935), 46–52. *Bio F J M Q*

———— "Techniques," *The Southern Review*, I, 1 (July 1935), 22, 31. *Cf Ge S*

Freeman, John, *The Moderns,* London, Robert Scott, 1916, p. 228. *S*

Gabriel, Gilbert W., "New Plays on Broadway," *Cue,* February 11, 1950, p. 18. *Dr S*

Gale, Robert L., "Art Imagery in Henry James's Fiction," *American Literature,* XXIX, 1 (March 1957), 47–63. *Ge St*

———— "Freudian Imagery in James's Fiction," *The American Imago,* XI (1954), 184. *H Psy*

Garland, Robert, *New York Theatre Critics' Reviews 1950,* XI, 4 (February 6, 1950), 361. *Dr F Gr M S*

Geismar, Maxwell, *Writers in Crisis,* Boston, Houghton Mifflin Co., 1942, p. 172. *Cf U*

Gerould, Gordon Hall, *The Patterns of English and American Fiction,* Boston, Little, Brown and Co., 1942, p. 444. *Ge S*

Gibbs, Wolcott, *The New Yorker,* XXV, 51 (February 11, 1950), 44. *Dr Em F Go Gr Ha J Ja M N P Q*

Gilbert, Justin, " 'The Innocents' Lacks Impact," New York *Mirror,* December 26, 1961, p. 21. *Dr F Go Gr H Ho J M Psy Q*

Goddard, Harold C., "A Pre-Freudian Reading of *The Turn of the Screw,*" *Nineteenth-Century Fiction,* XII, 1 (June 1957), 3–36. *B Em F Go Gr H Ha Ho J M N P Psy Q S T*

Gosse, Edmund, *Aspects and Impressions,* London, Cassell and Company, Ltd., 1922, p. 38. *Ho Ja S*

Grabo, Carl H., *The Technique of the Novel,* New York, Charles Scribner's Sons, 1928, pp. 204–214. *Go S*

Greene, Graham, "Books in General," *The New Statesman and Nation,* XXXIX, 986 (January 28, 1950), 101–102. *Ge*

———— "Henry James," *The English Novelists,* ed. Derek Verschoyle, New York, Harcourt, Brace and Co., 1936, pp. 236, 240. *Ja M Th Q*

Hamilton, Clayton, *Materials and Methods of Fiction,* New York, The Baker and Taylor Co., 1908, pp. 147, 177–178. *Ho S St Te*

Hart, James D., *The Oxford Companion to American Literature,* London, Oxford University Press, 1941, p. 365. *A*

Hawkins, William, *New York Theatre Critics' Reviews 1950,* XI, 4 (February 6, 1950), 361. *Am Dr Ge*

Haycraft, Howard, ed., *American Authors* (with Kunitz, Stanley J., ed.), New York, The H. W. Wilson Co., 1938, p. 412. *St*

————, "The Lure of the Demonic: James and Dürrenmatt," *Comparative Literature,* XIII, 4 (Fall 1961) 348–357. *A Cf Do Gr J M Psy Pv Q Te Th*

Heilman, Robert B., "The Freudian Reading of *The Turn of the Screw*," *MLN*, LXII (November 7, 1947), 433–445. *A Am F Go Gr H J M P Psy Te Th St*

———— "*The Turn of the Screw* as Poem," *The University of Kansas City Review*, XIV, 4 (Summer 1948), 277–289. *A F Ge Go Gr H J M Q T Th*

Hicks, Granville, *The Great Tradition*, New York, The Macmillan Co., 1935, p. 117. *Ge*

Hoffman, Charles G., "Innocence and Evil in James's *The Turn of the Screw*," *The University of Kansas City Review*, XX, 2 (Winter 1953), 98–105. *A F Go Gr H J Ja M Q T*

———— *The Short Novels of Henry James*, New York, Bookman Associates, 1957, pp. 6, 47, 70–96, 97–98, 99, 108–109, 115, 124. *A Am Cf Go Gr H J M O Q St Te Th*

Hogarth, Basil, *The Technique of Novel Writing*, London, John Lane, 1934, p. 164. *Na St*

Hueffer, Ford Madox. See Ford, Ford Madox.

Hughes, Helen S., *The History of the Novel in England* (with Robert Morss Lovett), Boston, Houghton Mifflin Co., 1932, p. 340. *A F Ho M Th*

Illustrated London News, The, CXIII (1898), 834. *Ho S*

———— CCXXV, 6027 (October 23, 1954), 713. *Dr Ge*

Independent, The, "The Two Magics," LI, 2614 (January 5, 1899), 73. *F Ho J M Q S U*

Ives, C. B., "James's Ghosts in *The Turn of the Screw*," *Nineteenth-Century Fiction*, XVIII, 2 (September 1963) 183–189. *F Gr J Ln M O Q*

James, Henry, *The Novels and Tales*, New York, Charles Scribner's Sons, 1908, V, p. xvi; XII, pp. xiv–xxii; XVII, p. xx. *F J Ja M Q*

Jefferson, D. W., *Henry James*, New York, Grove Press, Inc., 1961, p. 107. *Am Ha*

Jennings, Richard, "Fair Comment," *Nineteenth Century*, CXXXIII, 795 (May 1943), 230. *U*

Jones, Alexander E., "Point of View in *The Turn of the Screw*," *PMLA*, LXXIV, 1 (March 1959), 112–122. *A Bio F Go Gr H Ha Ho J M O Psy Pv Te Th*

Jones, Howard Mumford, *Major American Writers* (with Ernest E. Leisy and Richard M. Ludwig), New York, Harcourt, Brace and Co., 1952, p. 1443. *Te*

Josephson, Matthew, *Portrait of the Artist as American*, New York, Harcourt, Brace and Co., 1930, p. 254. *Ge S*

Kenton, Edna, "Henry James to the Ruminant Reader: *The Turn of the Screw*," *The Arts*, VI, 5 (November 1924), 245–255. *F Go J Ja Ho M N Q*

Keown, Eric, "At the Play," *Punch*, CCXI, 5524 (November 6, 1946), 408. *Dr*

———— "At the Play," *Punch*, CCXXIII, 5831 (July 16, 1952), 127. *Dr*

Kerner, David, "A Note on *The Beast in the Jungle*," *The University of Kansas City Review*, XVII, 2 (Winter 1950), 115. *Am Ge H J Q*

Knight, Arthur, "Innocents Abroad," *Saturday Review*, XLIV, 51 (December 23, 1961), 38–39. *Am Dr F Go Gr H Ho M Q Te*

Knight, Grant C., *American Literature and Culture*, New York, Ray Long and Richard R. Smith, Inc., 1932, p. 384. *Ho*

———— *The Novel in English*, New York, Richard R. Smith, Inc., 1931, pp. 278, 286. *Bio F Ge H M St U*

———— *Superlatives*, New York, Alfred A. Knopf, 1925, pp. 143, 145, 150. *F J Ja M Na Q S*

Krook, Dorothea, *The Ordeal of Consciousness in Henry James*, Cambridge, The Cambridge University Press, 1962, pp. 106–134, 370–389. *A Cf F Go Gr J M Pv Q Th*

Kunitz, Stanley J. See Haycraft, Howard.

Lanier, Henry Wysham, "Fiction, Poetry, and the Lighter Note in the Season's Books," *The American Monthly: Review of Reviews*, XVIII, 6 (December 1898), 732–733. *F Ho J M S Q*

Leach, Anna, "Henry James: An Appreciation," *The Forum*, LV, 5 (May 1916), 551–564. *Ho Ja S*

Leavis, F. R., "The Appreciation of Henry James," *Scrutiny*, XIV, 3 (Spring 1947), 229–237. *A U*

———— *The Great Tradition*, Garden City, Doubleday and Co., Inc., 1954, p. 194. *A Ge*

———— "Henry James and the Function of Criticism," *Scrutiny*, XV, 2 (Spring 1948), 98–104. *A Ge U*

———— "James's 'What Maisie Knew'," *Scrutiny*, XVII, 2 (Summer 1950), 115–118. *A Am F Go Gr J Ja M P Q U*

Leavis, Q. D., "Henry James: The Stories," *Scrutiny*, XIV, 3 (Spring 1947), 223–229. *Ja H Ha Ln*

———— "The Institution of Henry James," *Scrutiny*, XV, 1 (December 1947), 68–74. *A H*

Leisy, Ernest E. See Jones, Howard Mumford.

Levin, Harry, *The Power of Blackness*, New York, Vintage Books, 1960, p. 64. *Te Th*

Levy, Leo B., *"The Turn of the Screw* as Retaliation," *College English*, XVII, 5 (February 1956), 286–288. *Am Bio Cf Go H Ha Ja Q St*
———— *Versions of Melodrama: A Study of the Fiction of Henry James, 1865–1897*, Berkeley, University of California Press, 1957, p. 31. *Ge*

Lewis, Eugene, "Turning 'The Screw' into Opera," The Dallas *Times Herald*, February 21, 1963, p. 12. *A Dr F Go Gr J Ln M Psy Q*

Lewisohn, Ludwig, *The Story of American Literature*, New York, The Modern Library, 1939, pp. 264, 269. *S Th*

Liddell, Robert, *Some Principles of Fiction*, London, Jonathan Cape, 1953, p. 66. *Ge*
———— *A Treatise on the Novel*, London, Jonathan Cape, 1955, pp. 32, 71, 108, 138–145. *A Go H J Ja M Q S*

Liljegren, S. B., *American and European in the Works of Henry James*, Lund, Lunds Universitets Arsskrift, 1920, pp. 45, 50–51. *Go H M O*

Linn, James W., *A Foreword to Fiction* (with H. W. Taylor), New York, D. Appleton- Century Co., Inc. 1935, pp. 66, 192. *Ge St*

Literary World, The (Boston), XXIX, 23 (November 12, 1898), 367. *Ho*

Literary World, The (London), LVIII, 1519 (December 9, 1898), 456. *A F Ge Go Ho J M Q*

Living Age, The, CCCX, 4021 (July 30, 1921), 270. *F M*

Lovett, Robert Morss. See Hughes, Helen S.

Lubbock, Percy, *The Letters of Henry James*, London, Macmillan and Co., Ltd., 1920, pp. 286–287, 304, 306, 308, 416. *F Go Ja M O*

Ludwig, Richard M. See Jones, Howard Mumford.

Lydenberg, John, "The Governess Turns the Screw," *Nineteenth-Century Fiction*, XII, 1 (June 1957), 37–58. *Go J Ja Q Th*

McCarthy, Harold T., *Henry James: The Creative Process*, New York, Thomas Yoseloff, 1958, pp. 107, 110. *Am J Q Te Th*

Macdonald, Dwight, "The Innocents," *Esquire*, LVII, 341 (April 1962), 24. *Dr F Go Ho M St*

Machen, Arthur, "Arthur Machen Pays Tribute," *Mark Twain Quarterly*, V, 4 (1943), p. 8. *S*

Macy, John, *The Spirit of American Literature*, Garden City, New York, Doubleday, Page & Co., 1913, p. 334. *Go U*

Male, Roy R., Jr., "The Dual Aspects of Evil in 'Rappaccini's Daughter'," *PMLA*, LXIX, 1 (March 1954), 101. *Cf Go Th*

Marshall, Margaret, "Drama," *The Nation,* February 11, 1950, pp. 140–141. *Dr Ge Go Gr Ln P S*

Matthiessen, Francis O., *Henry James: The Major Phase,* New York, Oxford University Press, 1944, pp. 93–94, 140. *Cf F M Psy Th*

―――― *Henry James: Stories of Writers and Artists,* New York, New Directions, 1944, p. 9. *A Ja*

――――*The James Family,* New York, Alfred A. Knopf, 1947, pp. 112, 513. *St*

―――― *The Notebooks of Henry James* (with Kenneth B. Murdock), New York, Oxford University Press, 1947, pp. xiv, xvii, 18, 20, 28, 35–36, 40, 42, 49–50, 179. *A Ja O*

Mégroz, R. L., *Walter de la Mare,* London, Hodder and Stroughton, 1924, pp. 179–181. *A Cf J Psy Q St Te Th*

Milano, Paolo, *Henry James o il proscritto volontario,* Arnoldo Mondadori Editore, 1948, pp. 111–114. *A Cf St Te Th*

Miner, Earl Roy, "Henry James's Metaphysical Romances," *Nineteenth-Century Fiction,* IX, 1 (June 1954), 1–21. *A Bio Cf F Go Gr Ho Ja J M Psy Q Te Th*

Mortimer, Raymond, "Henry James," *Horizon,* VII, 41 (May 1943), 314–329. *Bio Ge Ja*

Munsey's Magazine, "Literary Chat," XX, 5 (February 1899), 820–823. *S St*

Murdock, Kenneth B. See Matthiessen, Francis O.

Nation, The, LXVII, 1745 (December 8, 1898), 432. *Ge Ho*

Newsweek, XXXV, 7 (February 13, 1950), 80–81. *Dr Ge*

New York Times, The, "Clayton's The Innocents," December 24, 1961, p. 9. *Am Dr Go*

―――― "Ingrid Bergman on TV," October 4, 1958, pp. 76, 77. *Dr Go Ha Psy*

―――― "A Star at Work," October 18, 1959, p. X 19, Sec. 2. *A Am Dr F Go Gr M*

―――― "TV: Powerful Portrayal," October 21, 1959, p. 87, col. 4. *A F Go Gr J M Q*

New York Times Magazine, The, December 3, 1961, p. 86. *A Dr*

Northrup, Clark Sutherland, "The Novelists," *A Manual of American Literature,* ed. Theodore Stanton, New York and London, G. P. Putnam's Sons, 1909, p. 194. *Cf Ho*

Nowell-Smith, Simon, *The Legend of the Master,* London, Constable and Co., Ltd., 1947, pp. 131–132. *Ja*

Nuhn, Ferner, *The Wind Blew from the East,* New York, Harper and Brothers, 1940, pp. 138, 140–141. *Ge H Ja*

Orage, A. R., "Henry James and the Ghostly," *The Little Review Anthology,* New York, Hermitage House, Inc., 1953, pp. 230–232. *Ge*

Outlook, The, "Books and Authors," LX, 9 (October 29, 1898), 536–544. *A Ge S*

——— "The Season's Books," LX, 14 (December 3, 1898), 875–884. *A S St*

Pelswick, Rose, "The Innocents," New York *Journal American,* December 26, 1961, p. 16. *Dr F Go Gr J Ja M Psy Q*

Penzoldt, Peter, *The Supernatural in Fiction,* London, Peter Nevill, Ltd., 1952, pp. 218–223. *Cf Ja N O S U*

Phelan, Kappo, "The Innocents," *The Commonweal,* LI, 19 (February 17, 1950), 509–510. *Dr Ge Ja*

Phelps, William Lyon, "Henry James—America's Analytical Novelist," *The Ladies' Home Journal,* XL, 11 (November 1923), 23, 174–175. *Ge Ho S*

——— *Howells, James, Bryant and Other Essays,* New York, The Macmillan Co., 1924, pp. 141–145. *S Te*

Porter, Katherine Anne, Allen Tate, and Mark Van Doren, "James: *The Turn of the Screw,*" *New Invitation to Learning,* ed. Mark Van Doren, New York, Random House, 1942, pp. 221–235. *A Do F Go Gr J H Ha Ln M N P Psy Pv Q S Te Th*

Pound, Ezra, *Instigations,* New York, Boni and Liveright, 1920, pp. 107, 150. *St U*

Powys, John Cowper, "John Cowper Powys on Henry James," *The Little Review Anthology,* New York, Hermitage House, Inc., 1953, pp. 28–30. *Ge*

Pratt, Cornelia Atwood, "The Evolution of Henry James," *The Critic,* XXXIV, 862 (April 1899), p. 341. *S St*

Preston, Harriet Waters, "The Latest Novels of Howells and James," *The Atlantic Monthly,* XCI, 543 (January 1903), 77–82. *Cf Ho Th*

Pritchard, John Paul, *Criticism in America,* Norman, University of Oklahoma Press, 1956, p. 275. *Ge Psy*

Quinn, Arthur Hobson, *American Fiction: An Historical and Critical Survey,* New York, D. Appleton-Century Co., 1936, pp. 294–295, 303. *A Go*

——— "Some Phases of the Supernatural in American Literature," *PMLA,* XXV, 1 (1910), pp. 132–133. *Cf S*

Rahv, Philip, *The Great Short Novels of Henry James,* New York, Dial Press, Inc., 1950, pp. 623–625. *Ge H Ja*

Reed, Glenn A., "Another Turn on James's 'The Turn of the Screw'," *American Literature,* XX, 4 (January 1949), 413–423. *A Bio Do Em Gr J Na P Q*

Reid, Charles, "At the Opera," *Punch,* CCXXVII, 5952 (October 13, 1954), 487. *Dr Ge*

Reid, Forrest, *Walter de la Mare,* London, Faber and Faber, Ltd., 1929, pp. 221–223. *A Cf S*

Richardson, Lyon N., *Henry James,* New York, American Book Company, 1941, pp. lxxxiv–lxxxv. *A Go J M Q*

Roberts, Morris, "Henry James," *The Sewanee Review,* LVII, 3 (Summer 1949), 521–525. *Ge Ha Ja Ln*

Roellinger, Francis X., Jr., "Psychical Research and 'The Turn of the Screw'," *American Literature,* XX, 4 (January 1949), 405. *J Q*

Schonberg, Harold C., "Opera: 'Turn of the Screw' Presented," *The New York Times,* March 27, 1962, p. 15. *A Dr F Go Ho J M Q Te*

Schorer, Mark, *The Story,* New York, Prentice-Hall, Inc., 1950. *St Te*

Sherman, Stuart P., "The Aesthetic Idealism of Henry James," *The Question of Henry James,* ed. F. W. Dupee, New York, Henry Holt and Co., 1945, pp. 70–91. *F M*

Silver, John, "A Note on the Freudian Reading of 'The Turn of the Screw'," *American Literature,* XXIX, 2 (May 1957), 207–211. *F Go Gr H Ha J M N Psy Q T Te*

Smith, Janet Adam, *Henry James and Robert Louis Stevenson,* London, Rupert Hart-Davis, 1948, pp. 38–39. *B Cf Ge Go St*

Smith, Roland M., "Anglo-Saxon Spinsters and Anglo-Saxon Archers," *MLN,* LXIV, 5 (May 1949), 312–315. *Ge*

Snell, George, *The Shapers of American Fiction, 1798–1947,* New York, E. P. Dutton and Company, Inc., 1947, p. 120. *Cf*

Spender, Stephen, *The Destructive Element,* London, Jonathan Cape, Ltd., 1935, pp. 34–35, 53. *Am B Ge J Ja H Q*

Spiller, Robert E., "Henry James," *Eight American Authors,* ed. Floyd Stovall, New York, The Modern Language Association of America, 1956, pp. 412–413. *Ge*

Stallman, R. W., "The Sacred Rage: The Time-Theme in 'The Ambassadors'," *Modern Fiction Studies,* III, 1 (Spring 1957), 41–56. *Am Ge Ja*

Stevenson, Elizabeth, *The Crooked Corridor,* New York, The Macmillan Company, 1949, p. 139. *A F Go J M Q*

Stoll, Elmer Edgar, "Symbolism in Coleridge," *PMLA,* LXIII, 1 (March 1948), 230. *A H J Ja Q*

Stovall, Floyd, "Henry James's 'The Jolly Corner'," *Nineteenth-Century Fiction,* XII, 1 (June 1957), p. 82. *A Cf Go*

Sweeney, John L., "The Demuth Pictures," *Kenyon Review,* V, 4 (Autumn 1943), 522–532. *I*

Tate, Allen. See Porter, Katherine Anne.

Taylor, H. W. See Linn, James W.

Taylor, Walter Fuller, *A History of American Letters,* New York, American Book Co., 1936, p. 291. *Ge*

——— *The Story of American Letters,* Chicago, H. Regnery Co., 1956, pp. 265–266. *A Te*

Theatre Arts, "The Innocents," XXXIV, 4 (April 1950), 16. *Dr Ln P*

Thurber, James, "The Wings of Henry James," *The New Yorker,* XXXV, 38 (November 7, 1959), 188–201. *Dr Ja O Q S*

Time, "Evil Emanations," LXXIX, 1 (January 5, 1962), 59. *Am Dr Em F Go Gr H Ho M St Th*

——— "The Theatre," LV, 7 (February 13, 1950), 52–53. *A Am Dr F Go Gr Ha M Psy*

Times Literary Supplement, The (London), No. 2530 (July 28, 1950), 470. *Ge Ha St*

——— No. 2607 (January 18, 1952), 51. *A Ge Go Gr Ho Na*

Tindall, William York, *Forces in Modern British Literature,* New York, Vintage Books, 1956, p. 191. *Go Ha N*

Tintner, Adeline R., "The Spoils of Henry James," *PMLA,* LXI, No. 1, Part 1, (March 1946), 239–251. *Ge*

Trewin, J. C., "The World of the Theatre," *The Illustrated London News,* CCXXI, 5905 (July 19, 1952), 108. *Dr Ge*

Troy, William, "The Altar of Henry James," *The Question of Henry James,* ed. F. W. Dupee, New York, Henry Holt and Co., 1945, pp. 267–272. *Go H N*

TV Guide, V, 35 (August 29, 1959), p. A–i. *Dr*

Updike, John, "Beerbohm and Others," *The New Yorker,* XXXVII, 31 (September 16, 1961), 173. *St*

Uzzell, Thomas H., *The Technique of the Novel,* New York, J. B. Lippincott, 1947, p. 285. *Ge Go S St*

Vaid, Krishna Baldev, *Technique in the Tales of Henry James,* Cambridge, Harvard University Press, 1964, pp. 90–122. *A Am F Gr H J M Pv Q Te*

Van Doren, Carl, *The American Novel,* New York, The Macmillan Company, 1921, p. 210. *A Am F H M Th*
—— Introduction to *The Turn of the Screw,* The Heritage Press, 1949, pp. ix–xiv. *A F Go Gr H Ha I J Ja M Q S*
Van Doren, Mark. See Porter, Katherine Anne.
Variety, CCXXV, 2 (December 6, 1961), 6. *A Do Dr Go Gr H Ho J Psy Q*
—— CCXXVIII, 8 (October 17, 1962), 57. *Am Ho*
Walbrook, H. M., "The Novels of Henry James," *Fortnightly Review,* CXXVII (May 1930), 680–691, 761. *Ge St*
Waldock, A. J. A., "Mr Edmund Wilson and *The Turn of the Screw,*" *MLN,* LXII, 5 (May 1947), 332–333. *A Go Gr H Q*
Walpole, Hugh, "England," *Tendencies of the Modern Novel,* London, George Allen and Unwin, Ltd., 1934, p. 17. *Bio J Q Te*
Ward, Alfred C., *Aspects of the Modern Short Story,* London, University of London Press, 1924, pp. 90–101. *Cf H J Ja O Q S St*
Ward, J. A., *The Imagination of Disaster: Evil in the Fiction of Henry James,* Lincoln, University of Nebraska Press, 1961, pp. 16–17, 56, 64, 66–72, 79–80, 88, 176. *A Cf F Go M Psy Th*
Watts, Richard, Jr., "The Case of the Haunted Children," *New York Theatre Critics' Reviews 1950,* XI, 4, February 6, 1950, p. 359. *A Dr Ge*
Wescott, Glenway, "A Sentimental Contribution," *The Hound and Horn,* VII, 3 (April–May 1934), 523–534. *Ge H*
West, Katharine, *Chapter of Governesses: A Study of the Governess in English Fiction, 1800–1949,* London, Cohen and West, 1949, pp. 179–182. *A F Go M U*
West, Rebecca, *Henry James,* New York, Henry Holt and Co., 1916, pp. 97–98. *F Go J M S Q*
Wharton, Edith, *The Writing of Fiction,* New York, Charles Scribner's Sons, 1925, p. 40. *A Ge Go Ho J S Q*
Willen, Gerald, ed., *A Casebook on Henry James's "The Turn of the Screw,"* New York, Thomas Y. Crowell Company, 1960. (Contains many of James's own comments on *The Turn of the Screw* and fifteen articles treating almost every conceivable facet of the novel.)
Wilson, Edmund, "The Ambiguity of Henry James," *Hound and Horn,* VII, 3 (April–May 1934), 385–406. *Am F Go J M N P Psy*
—— "The Ambiguity of Henry James," *The Triple Thinkers,* New York, Harcourt, Brace and Company, 1938, pp. 122–164. *Am F Go J M N P Psy*

———— "A Treatise on Tales of Horror," *The New Yorker,* XX, 15 (May 27, 1944), 72. *A Go Ja Psy*

Wilson, Harris W., "What *Did* Maisie Know?" *College English,* XVII, 5 (February 1956), 279. *Cf Psy*

Winsten, Archer, "The Innocents," New York *Post,* December 26, 1961, p. 24. *A Dr F Go Gr H J M Q*

Winters, Yvor, *In Defense of Reason,* Denver, The University of Denver Press, 1947, pp. 316–317, 331. *Em F Ge Go H Ha Ja M N*

Wolff, Robert Lee, "The Genesis of 'The Turn of the Screw'," *American Literature,* XIII, 1 (March 1941), 1–8. *H I Ja Ln O St*

Worsley, T. C., "The Massacre of the Innocents," *The New Statesman and Nation,* XLIV, 1114 (July 12, 1952), 39–40. *Dr Go*

Zabel, Morton D., *The Portable Henry James,* New York, The Viking Press, 1951, pp. 213, 695. *Ge H Ln*

INDEX

Admirable Crichton, The: 111

"Ambiguity of Henry James, The": as nonapparitionist interpretation, 22, 94; mentioned, 99

Amelia: governess' reading of, 25, 39, 165

Andreas, Osborn: nonapparitionist interpretation of, 7–8; on governess' relation with children, 30; on governess as danger to children, 169

apparitionist interpretation. SEE *Turn of the Screw, The,* apparitionist-nonapparitionist debate on

"Appearance and Reality in Henry James": 8

"Architecture of Henry James's 'New York Edition,' The": 6

Arnold, Thomas: as headmaster, 74–75; mentioned, 149

Arts, The: 5

Aspern Papers, The: 6–7

bachelor of Harley Street. SEE uncle (bachelor of Harley Street)

Beers, Henry A.: nonapparitionist interpretation of, 5

Brewer, Josef: 36

Bamford, T. W.: 74

Bewley, Marius: nonapparitionist interpretation of, 8–9; on Flora's denial of seeing ghost, 156

Britten, Benjamin: opera of, 40

Broun, Heywood: 22

Brown, John Mason: on James's intent, 12

caste system, English. SEE social hierarchy, English

Cargill, Oscar: on James's psychology, 35–36; on governess' description of Quint, 99

Casebook on Henry James's "The Turn of the Screw," A: 9, 99

"Case of Miss Lucy R., The": as James's source, 36

Chapter of Governesses: A Study of the Governess in English Fiction, 1800–1949: 151

Charcot, Jean Martin: and James, 35

children, the: in apparitionist interpretation, 4–5; in nonapparitionist interpretation, 6, 7–8; social station of, 107, 110; relationship between, 26, 98, 162, 164; cleverness of, 150–151; letters of, to uncle, 153, 154, 163; mentioned, 9, 14, 22, 26, 46, 70, 87, 124, 143. SEE ALSO Flora; Grose, Mrs., and children; Miles

——, relation of, with governess: in nonapparitionist interpretation, 7–8; governess' autobiographical stories in, 25, 161; governess' emotional needs in, 28–29, 30; governess' demonstrations of affection in, 29; and governess' relation with uncle, 47–48; Flora's silence in, 51; in governess' nonseizural attacks, 56–57; governess on children's communing with ghosts in, 56–57, 69, 79, 82–84, 95–96, 123, 129–132, 143, 144, 147, 152, 155, 156, 162, 166–167, 168; in governess' seventh seizure, 61–66 *passim,* 144, 147, 156, 167; children's relation with Quint and Miss Jessel in, 67, 112–114; in governess' eighth seizure, 69, 88, 167–168; governess' inductions from children's behavior in, 82–83; as foil for governess' martyrdom, 89–92; and moonlight episode, 94–98, 165–167; governess' nocturnal activities in, 97, 157; children's affection for governess in, 98; governess' authority over children in, 107, 108; governess' promise to keep experience from children in, 136–137, 145–146, 155–156; children's agreement to humor governess in, 138–139; governess teacher in, 148–151; governess' surveillance in, 150, 158–159, 162, 164; children's suffering from governess' behavior in, 151–155, 157–169; children's efforts to help governess in, 153, 161–164, 165–166; and governess' accusations against children, 152, 156; governess' treatment of letters to uncle in, 154, 163; in church scene, 155; and children's concern for governess, 157, 164–165; and governess' insane looks and noises, 159–161; and governess' awareness of children's perception, 163–164; and governess' coarseness, 164–165; and children's revulsion against governess, 167–168

—, relation of, to Quint and Miss Jessel: in apparitionist interpretation, 4, 5; as ghosts, 56–57, 69, 79, 82–84, 95–96, 123, 129–132, 143, 144, 147, 152, 155, 156, 157, 162, 166–167, 168; as mystification tormenting governess, 67; in past, 67, 108, 112–113, 131–132; governess as jealous of, 108

Collier's: 3, 36

Critic, The: 5

Douglas: on governess' background and character, 23–24, 31; on governess' emotional instability, 31; on governess' love for uncle, 42–43; on governess' authority, 107; on Miss Jessel's character reference, 128; mentioned, 21, 74, 148

Dupee, F. W: no James's comments on *TS,* 12–13

Edel, Leon: on Goddard's essay, 5; on Kenton's interpretation, 5–6; on James's classification of *TS,* 6–7; on James's intentions, 10, 34–35; on effect of *TS* revisions on tone, 18; on three levels of *TS,* 34–35; on James's psychological knowledge, 35; on governess' curiosity, 86; mentioned, 16, 36

Edgar, Pelham: apparitionist interpretation of, 4

Elton, Oliver: nonapparitionist interpretation of, 5

Evans, Oliver: on apparitionist-nonapparitionist debate, 4; apparitionist interpretation of, 7, 169; on James's

intentions, 10; on governess' basic stability, 33; on James on governess' authority, 107

Fielding, Henry: 25, 39

Firebaugh, Joseph J.: on Quint-Miles relationship, 112

Five Kinds of Writing: 22

Flora: denies seeing ghosts, 61, 156, 162; as source of governess' information, 99; efforts of, to divert governess, 153; mentioned, 24, 32, 40, 43, 54, 68, 71, 74, 128, 137. SEE ALSO children

Freud, Sigmund: on writers' psychological insight, 35; as James's source, 36

Fromm, Eric: 89

Ghostly Tales, The: 34, 86

ghosts: in apparitionist interpretation, 4–5, 7; in nonapparitionist interpretation, 5, 6, 8. SEE ALSO hallucinations; governess, seizures of; Quint, Peter, and Miss Jessel

Gibbs, Woolcott: on nonapparitionist interpretation, 35, 94; mentioned, 98

Goddard, Harold C.: nonapparitionist interpretation of, 5; on governess' desire for martyrdom, 90; on moonlight episode, 96; on Mrs. Grose's identification of Quint, 99, 105; on governess' looks and noises, 159, 160

Goody Gosling: 25

✳ governess, the: in apparitionist-non-apparitionist interpretations, 4–9; as point of view of *TS,* 5–6, 8; prologue in interpreting, 6; James's revisions on reactions of, 18–20; explanation of images of, 44–46; authority of, 107–109; SEE ALSO children, relation of, with governess; Grose, Mrs., relations of, with governess

—, character of: critical comment on, 4–9, 30–31, 32–33; emotional needs in, 7–8, 28–30; James's comments on, 14–15; prologue on, 23, 28, 30, 31; effect of background on, 23–30, 31–33; effect of poverty on, 24–25; effect of father on, 25–27, 28; attitude toward men in, 26; tendency to suspect evil in, 26–27, 82; basic instability of, 31–33; curiosity in, 86–